KNOWING AND DOING
THE WILL OF GOD

Knowing and Doing the Will of God

J.I. Packer

Compiled by LaVonne Neff

VINE
BOOKS

Servant Publications
Ann Arbor, Michigan

Vine Books is an imprint of Servant Publications
especially designed to serve evangelical Christians.

Scripture used in the work, unless otherwise indicated, is taken from the HOLY
BIBLE: NEW INTERNATIONAL VERSION.® NIV® © 1973, 1978, 1984 by
the International Bible Society. Used by permission of Zondervan Publishing
House.

Excerpts from *Concise Theology*, © 1987 by J.I. Packer. Used by permission of
Tyndale House Publishers, Inc. All rights reserved. Excerpts from *Hot Tub
Religion*, © 1993 by Foundation for Reformation. Used by permission of Tyndale
House Publishers, Inc. All rights reserved. Excerpts from *God's Words*, © 1988 by
J.I. Packer. Used by permission of Baker Book House Company. Excerpts from
Evangelism and the Sovereignty of God by J.I. Packer. © 1961 by InterVarsity
Fellowship. Used by permission of InterVarsity Press, P.O. Box 1400, Downers
Grove, IL 60515. Excerpts from *Growing in Christ* by J.I. Packer © 1994. Used
by permission of Good News Publishers/Crossway Books, Wheaton, Illinois,
60187. Excerpts from *A Passion for Faithfulness* by J.I. Packer, 1995. Used by per-
mission of Good News Publishers/Crossway Books, Wheaton, Illinois 60187.

Published by Servant Publications
P.O. Box 8617
Ann Arbor, Michigan 48107

00 01 02 03 04 05   6 5 4 3 2

Printed in the United States of America
ISBN 1-56955-220-7

Library of Congress Cataloging-in-Publication Data

Packer, J.I. (James Innel)
    Knowing and doing the will of God / J.I. Packer : compiled by
Lavonne Neff.
        p.   cm.
    Includes bibliographical references
    ISBN 0-89283-927-9
    1. Devotional calendars.   2. Christian life—meditations.
I. Neff, Lavonne.   II. Title.
BV4811.P23   1995
242'.2—dc20

                                                                95-14298
                                                                     CIP

Contents

On a sugar packet often found in American restaurants appears this wisecrack: "Experience is a wonderful thing. It enables you to recognize a mistake when you make it again." Ha, as some of my friends would say. But the cynical dictum has a more cheerful flip side: experience equips you to identify not only failures but successes too. Like this book.

For me to say that might seem an outrageous tooting of my own horn, but really it is not so. For, in the deepest sense, I did not write this book at all. The sentences and paragraphs are certainly mine, but it is the selection and arrangement that makes *Knowing and Doing the Will of God* what it is, and with that I had nothing to do. For the second time in my life, a recurring theme was found in my published work, someone followed it up, and there emerged a daily devotional.

LaVonne Neff is the person who did the work, and I cannot sufficiently applaud her skill. She has arranged these pickings from Packer in a way that welds the year's readings into a full-orbed declaration of life in Christ, and has thus produced a book from which I myself could, and I guess should, draw help in my own stumbling attempts to walk with God. Thank you, LaVonne, and may the brilliant job you have done bring vision and strength from God to many in these daunting days.

J. I. Packer

JANUARY

God guides those who
want to do his will.

When I consider your heavens,
the work of your fingers,
the moon and the stars,
which you have set in place,
what is man that you are mindful of him,
the son of man that you care for him?

Psalm 8:3-4

What is man? It is an inescapable question which no one who thinks at all can avoid asking about himself or herself. We can stand back from ourselves and look at ourselves and judge ourselves and ask basic questions about ourselves, and, what is more, we cannot help doing these things. The questions ask themselves, unbidden; willy-nilly, one finds oneself wondering what life means, what sense it makes, what one is here for. Am I a hero, a victim, or just a nonentity in the world of which I am consciously part? How should I value myself? And how should I direct myself? How should I make decisions at crunch points in life? Does life's ultimate frustration and waste consist in the fact that none of the things that seem important to us really mean anything? Is life, after all, a tale told by an idiot, full of sound and fury, signifying nothing? Again I ask: what is man? For thinking people, the question is inescapable.

"A Christian View of Man," 104-107

REFLECT: What is the meaning of my life?

The length of our days is seventy years—
or eighty, if we have the strength;
yet their span is but trouble and sorrow,
for they quickly pass, and we fly away.

Psalm 90:10

More questions arise: the question of *identity*, for instance. Who are you? You don masks, you play roles; how, amid all that, can you identify, and identify with, the real you? Again, there is the question of *goals*. Has life a purpose? If so, which way should I go to fulfill it? That raises the question of *destiny*. What am I here for? What can I hope for? Intimations of immortality come to us all; the atheist resolutely squelches them; dare we trust them? If we do, we next must ask whether what we do now will affect what we experience then. In any case, we all have to die some day, and that brings up the question whether my future death will make nonsense of my life.

"A Christian View of Man," 107

REFLECT: Where is my life going?

As the deer pants for streams of water,
so my soul pants for you, O God.

Psalm 42:1

Does any concern command more interest or arouse more anxiety among modern Bible-believers than discovering the will of God? I do not think so. The desire to know God's guidance is a sign of spiritual health. Healthy believers want to please God. Through the great change of heart that we call regeneration they have come to love obedience and to find joy in doing God's will, and the very thought of offending him grieves them deeply. To live in a way that shows gratitude to God for his grace is their purpose, indeed their passion, and as they grow spiritually, this desire becomes stronger. Naturally, therefore, they want as clear indications of the will of God as they can get, so that they may do it.

"Wisdom along the Way," 20

REFLECT: Healthy Christians long to know God's will.

I have not spoken in secret,
from somewhere in a land of darkness; ...
I, the LORD, speak the truth;
I declare what is right.

Isaiah 45:19

A feeling of bewilderment swamps most modern Westerners at the vast range of choices in every field that our civilization opens to us. A wish for help in decision making is an understandable reaction. Some would rely for this on gurus, palmists, astrologers, clairvoyants, Ann Landers, and specialist counselors. Healthy Christians, however, while valuing human advice, look to God also. There are, after all, in Scripture many promises of divine direction, and many testimonies to its reality in the lives of biblical saints, in light of which it would be positively wrong for a Christian not to seek God's help in making choices, commitments, and other decisions.

"Wisdom along the Way," 20

REFLECT: God promises to help with decisions.

Then the LORD answered Job out of the storm. He said: "Who is this that darkens my counsel with words without knowledge?"
Job 38:1-2

I find that the more earnest and sensitive a believer is, the more likely he or she is to be hung up somewhere about guidance. Why is this? we ask. The answer does not seem to be far to seek. The source of anxiety is threefold: a desire for guidance, uncertainty about how to get it, and fear of the consequences of not getting it.

Such anxiety has an unhappy way of escalating. Anxious people get allured by any and every form of certainty that offers itself, no matter how irrational; they become vulnerable to strange influences and do zany things. Over the past 150 years there has been a most unhelpful buildup of tension, to a point where it muddles minds, darkens counsel, and obstructs maturity in a way that is Spirit-quenching and scandalous.

"Wisdom along the Way," 19

REFLECT: Anxiety about God's will can lead to muddled thinking and foolish behavior.

I will repay you for the years the locusts have eaten.... You will have plenty to eat, until you are full, and you will praise the name of the LORD your God, who has worked wonders for you.
Joel 2:25-26

The fear of spiritual ruin through mistaking God's guidance is a sign of unthinking unbelief. I have met this particular fear many times in my ministry. It may be stated as follows: *God's plan for your life is like an itinerary drawn up for you as if by a travel agent. As long as you are in the right place at the right time to board each plane or train or bus or boat, all is well. But the moment you miss one of these preplanned connections, the itinerary is ruined. A new one may then be devised, but it can only ever be second best compared with the original perfect plan.* The assumption is that God lacks either the will or the wisdom or both to get you back on track; therefore a substandard spiritual life is all that is open to you now. Your one mistake sentences you to live and serve God as a second-rate Christian forever.

Such a fear expresses unbelief regarding the goodness, wisdom, and power of God, who can and does restore the years that the locusts have eaten.

"Wisdom along the Way," 20

REFLECT: It is never too late to get back on track with God.

Who can discern his errors?
Forgive my hidden faults.
Keep your servant also from willful sins;
may they not rule over me.
Then will I be blameless,
innocent of great transgression.

Psalm 19:12-13

It is true that ordinarily one has to live with the human and material consequences of the decisions one makes, and bad decisions have sad consequences from which we cannot expect to be shielded. But Scripture shows us a number of saints making great and grievous mistakes about the will of God for them—Jacob fooling his father, Moses murdering the Egyptian, David numbering the people, Peter boycotting Gentile believers, for example—yet none of them thereby became incurably second-class. On the contrary, they were each forgiven and restored, which in fact is how all true saints live all the time. Misconceiving God's will is surely less sinful than knowing it and not doing it, and if God restored David after his adultery with Bathsheba and his eliminating of Uriah, and Peter after his threefold denial of Christ, we should not doubt that he can and will restore Christians who err only through making honest mistakes about his guidance.

"Wisdom along the Way," 20-21

REFLECT: It is better to make an honest mistake than to do nothing for fear of making a mistake.

The secret things belong to the LORD our God, but the things revealed belong to us and to our children forever, that we may follow all the words of this law.

Deuteronomy 29:29

Some seek guidance by making their minds blank and receiving what then rises into consciousness as a divine directive. This undoubtedly keeps people honest with their own consciences, often to good effect. But murky urges and self-indulgent dreams, as well as pricks from conscience, will surface at such times, and those who assume that whatever "vision" fills the blank is from God have no defense against the invasion of obsessive, grandiose, self-serving imaginations spawned by our own conceit.

Others, like the diviners of ancient paganism and the devotees of modern astrology, hope to be told facts about the future in the light of which they may chart a knowledgeable course in the present. This is what guidance means to their minds. But Scripture directs us to live by God's revealed will of precept, rather than by any such pryings into his hidden will of purpose.

"Wisdom along the Way," 22

REFLECT: God may not tell me what he is planning, but he lets me know how he wants me to live.

This is what each of you keeps on saying to his friend or relative: "What is the LORD's answer?" or "What has the LORD spoken?" But you must not mention "the oracle of the LORD" again, because every man's own word becomes his oracle and so you distort the words of the living God, the LORD Almighty, our God.

Jeremiah 23:35-36

Whenever in our quest for God's guidance we lose theological control, erratic superstitions take us over. To start with, we isolate and narrow the guidance issue as if it relates only to major decisions that involve sizable risks for the future, like the choice of a life partner, of a vocation and an employment, or of a place to live and work in one's calling. That isolation is a fruit of bad theology in itself, and opens the door to the further mistake of supposing that guidance regularly comes out of the blue, like an oracle reflecting facts about the future that we ourselves do not and cannot know. Those who look for guidance through a prophecy, inner voice, "fleece," or random selection of Bible verses are clearly under the spell of this misconception.

"Paths of Righteousness," 32

REFLECT: God's guidance rarely comes through spectacular means.

The Pharisees came and began to question Jesus. To test him, they asked him for a sign from heaven. He sighed deeply and said, "Why does this generation ask for a miraculous sign? I tell you the truth, no sign will be given to it."

Mark 8:11-12

Many Christians embrace the romantic fancy that all true guidance experiences can be reported in terms of the formula, "the Lord told me" thus and so; in other words, that they are all experiences producing absolute confidence about the rightness of one specific line of action. In the absence of such experience we say that we have not received guidance as yet. If, however, after prayer we find ourselves with a pressing urge in our minds, we hail it as "my guidance" and defy anyone to argue us out of it. Are we right? Probably not, either time. Yet this idea of guidance is so well established in our thinking that a recent book could call it the traditional view. Actually this idea of guidance is a novelty among orthodox evangelicals, not going back further than the last century. It has led good people to so much foolish action on the one hand, and so much foolish inaction on the other, and so much puzzlement and heartbreak when the hotline to God seemed to go silent, that it must by now be regarded as somewhat discredited.

"Paths of Righteousness," 32

REFLECT: Guidance does not mean certainty about a particular course of action.

When Gideon realized that it was the angel of the LORD, he exclaimed, "Ah, Sovereign LORD! I have seen the angel of the LORD face to face!" But the LORD said to him, "Peace! Do not be afraid. You are not going to die."

Judges 6:22-23

Scripture gives us no more warrant to expect hotline, voice-from-the-control-tower experiences of personal guidance than to expect new authoritative revelations to come to us for the guidance of the whole church. Certainly God's guidance is promised to every believer, and certainly some individuals in the Scripture stories (Gideon, Manoah and his wife, and Philip, for instance) received guidance in hotline fashion. But we must learn to distinguish between the ordinary and the extraordinary, the constant and the occasional, the rule and the exception. God may reveal himself and give guidance to his servants any way he pleases, and it is not for us to set limits to him. But one question is whether or not we are entitled to expect hotline disclosures on a regular basis. To this question, so I urge, the correct answer is no. All the biblical narratives of God's direct communications with men and women are on the face of it exceptional, and the biblical model of personal guidance is something quite different.

"Paths of Righteousness," 33-34

REFLECT: God does not usually use a hotline from heaven to give me guidance.

Dear friends, do not believe every spirit, but test the spirits to see whether they are from God, because many false prophets have gone out into the world.

1 John 4:1

If anyone today receives a direct disclosure from God on any matter at all, it will have *no canonical significance:* that is, it will not be meant to become part of the church's rule of faith and life, nor will the church as such be under any obligation to acknowledge the disclosure as revelation; nor will anyone merit blame for suspecting that the disclosure was not from God at all. If the alleged disclosure is a prediction, Moses assures us that there is not even a *prima facie* case for treating it as genuinely from God until it is seen to have come true (Deuteronomy 18:21-22). If the alleged disclosure is a directive (as when a leader claims that God told him to found a hospital or university or crusade of some kind), any who associate themselves with his project should do so because wisdom tells them that it is needed, realistic, and God-honoring, not because the leader tells them that God directly commanded him (and by implication them) to attempt it.

"True Guidance," 37-38

REFLECT: God rarely speaks directly to individuals today, and any claims of direct disclosure should be rigorously tested.

Whether you turn to the right or to the left, your ears will hear a voice behind you, saying, "This is the way; walk in it."

Isaiah 30:21

Part of what being Spirit-led means, some would tell us, is that one receives instructions from the Spirit through prophecies and inward revelations, as repeatedly happened to godly folk in Bible times. They would urge that communications of this kind are the fulfillment of God's promise in Isaiah 30:21. This verse, however, which at first seems to point this way, is actually promising a supply of wise teaching, not of inward voices speaking apart from what is written. Any, therefore, who believe that a direct revelation has been given them should not on this account expect such a thing ever to occur again; and the idea that specially holy persons may expect this sort of guidance often, or that such experiences are a proof of their holiness and of their call and fitness to lead others, should be dismissed out of hand. Guidance in this particular form is *not promised;* for it to occur is extraordinary, exceptional, and anomalous. No Scripture leads us either to hope for it or to look for it.

"True Guidance," 37-38

REFLECT: God is more likely to direct me through wise teaching than through inner voices.

My son, if you accept my words
and store up my commands within you,
turning your ear to wisdom
and applying your heart to understanding; ...
then you will understand the fear of the LORD
and find the knowledge of God.

Proverbs 2:1-2, 5

In making a decision, one invariable rule is that that which is merely good ("good enough," as we say) must never become the enemy of the best. It is never enough to ask, as the Pharisees did, whether such and such a course of action is free from taint of sin; the Christian's question should be, is it the best I can envisage for the glory of God and the good of souls? God enables us to discern this by prayerfully using our minds—thinking how Scripture applies, comparing alternatives, weighing advice, taking account of our heart's desire, estimating what we are capable of. Some might call this common sense, but the Bible calls it wisdom, and sees it as one of God's most precious gifts.

"Wisdom along the Way," 21

REFLECT: What is the best I can imagine in my present circumstance?

Now what I am commanding you today is not too difficult for you or beyond your reach. It is not up in heaven,... nor is it beyond the sea.... No, the word is very near you; it is in your mouth and in your heart so you may obey it.

Deuteronomy 30:11-14

Why do some Christians play down the significance of thought and wisdom in decision-making? There is a mixture of reasons:

- The anti-intellectual, feeling-oriented, short-term mentality of today's secular culture, invading and swamping Christian minds.
- An admirable humility: believers do not trust themselves to discern the ideal course of action, and hence long to have it directly revealed to them.
- The quite false idea that what God wants his children to do is irrational by ordinary standards, and not therefore something to which wisdom as such would direct us.
- The fancy that, since each Christian is a special object of God's love, special instructions from God can be expected.

God is sovereign, and very gracious to those who humbly seek him. No doubt he has on occasion given guidance by all the means I have mentioned, and no doubt he will again. But such cases are exceptions, and to expect them to be the rule is to ask for trouble.

"Wisdom along the Way," 22

REFLECT: Nothing can replace careful thinking in making wise decisions.

Examine yourselves to see whether you are in the faith; test your-selves. Do you not realize that Christ Jesus is in you—unless, of course, you fail the test?

2 Corinthians 13:5

Impressions—not ordinarily revelations of information, but rather focusings of concern—belong to the authentic reality of Christian living. When we say we have a "vision" or "burden" for something, we are testifying to an impression, and when our concern is biblically proper we are right to treat our impression as a nudge from the Holy Spirit. Yet all impressions must be rigorously tested by appeal to biblical wisdom—the corporate wisdom of the believing community, as well as any personal wisdom one has—lest impressions that are rooted in egoism, pride, headstrong unrealism, a fancy that irrationality glorifies God, a sense that some human being is infallible, or any similar unhealthiness of soul, be allowed to masquerade as Spirit-given. Those who receive impressions about what they should believe and do ought therefore to suspect them, and suspect their own hearts as a possible source of them. Only impressions verified as biblical-ly appropriate and practically wise should be treated as com-ing from God.

"True Guidance," 39

REFLECT: If an impression agrees with biblical and practical wisdom, I can respond to it as to a nudge from the Holy Spirit.

Plans fail for lack of counsel,
but with many advisers they succeed.

Proverbs 15:22

God's guidance is more like the marriage guidance, child guidance, or career guidance that is received from counselors than it is like being talked down by the airport controller as one flies blind through the clouds. Seeking God's guidance is not like practicing divination or consulting oracles, astrologers, and clairvoyants for information about the future, but rather is comparable with our everyday thinking-through of alternative options in given situations to determine the best course open to us. The inward experience of being divinely guided is not ordinarily one of seeing signs or hearing voices, but rather one of being enabled to work out the best thing to do.

"Paths of Righteousness," 34

REFLECT: God will help me make sound decisions.

Do not conform any longer to the pattern of this world, but be transformed by the renewing of your mind. Then you will be able to test and approve what God's will is—his good, pleasing and perfect will.

Romans 12:2

Inward discernment of the best and holiest thing to do is always a fruit of faith, repentance, consecration, and transformation by the Holy Spirit. Familiar indeed is the first sentence of this verse. Less often, however, is stress laid on the second. "Test" means "discern by examining alternatives," and Paul's point is that there is a moral and spiritual precondition of being able in each situation to see what God wants done. Those whose minds God is currently transforming may still err about specific aspects of God's will, in areas of life where their residual unwisdom still holds sway, but where no work of inward renewal is in progress, no adequate discernment of God's will is to be expected at all. Guidance is God's gift to those who are looking to him—that means precisely, looking to Jesus Christ—to save them from sin.

"Paths of Righteousness," 36

REFLECT: God guides those he is saving from sin.

Wisdom will enter your heart,
and knowledge will be pleasant to your soul.
Discretion will protect you;
and understanding will guard you.
Wisdom will save you from the ways of wicked men.

Proverbs 2:10-12

Is there a personal touch from God when we choose a course of action? Most certainly. Those whom God wants in the pastorate, or in crosscultural missionary work, or some other specialized ministry, are ordinarily made to realize that they will never get job satisfaction doing anything else. When God has in mind a particular career for a person he ordinarily bestows an interest in that field of expertise. When God plans that two people should marry he ordinarily blends their hearts. But God's inclining of the heart (as distinct from our own self-generated ambitions and longings) are experienced only as meshing in with the judgments of wisdom. Thus, a passion for an unsuitable person as a life partner, or for a ministry beyond one's ability level, should be seen as a temptation rather than a divine call.

"Wisdom along the Way," 21

REFLECT: My particular passion can be either a temptation or a divine call.

The LORD is my shepherd, I shall not be in want. He makes me lie down in green pastures, he leads me beside quiet waters, he restores my soul.

Psalm 23:1-2

The classic Bible presentation of the guided life, and of the reality of the guidance that produces it, is surely Psalm 23, that beloved shepherd psalm. Christians should read it as a declaration of what it means to be a believer led through life by the God who is Father, Son, and Holy Spirit. The picture is of the saint as a divinely shepherded sheep. Silly and apt to stray as I am, my covenant God will not leave me bereft of either security or sustenance. He provides rest ("beside quiet waters"), refreshment ("he restores my soul"), protection ("through the valley of the shadow of death"), enrichment ("you prepare a table"), and enjoyment ("goodness and love will follow"). Guidance is one facet of that total covenant care whereby the King of Love draws me into the destiny of deliverance and delight that he planned out for me before the world was.

"Paths of Righteousness," 34-35

REFLECT: The Lord is *my* shepherd.

He guides me in paths of righteousness for his name's sake.

Psalm 23:3

"Paths of righteousness" are ways of behaving that are right, and please God, because they correspond to his command and match his moral nature. Vocational decisions that are perceptive and prudent are certainly included, but the basic idea is of being holy as our holy God calls us all to be, and this is where biblical guidance always centers. "For his name's sake" means for the furthering of his glory through his demonstration of covenant faithfulness. The Lord is my shepherd: he is pledged to watch over me, order my travels, stay with me, and bring me safely home, and he will not fail in his commitment. Finally, "he guides me" means that by his instruction within the frame of his providence he gives me wisdom to see the right thing—the best thing, the most fruitful thing, the purest and noblest thing, the most Christlike and God-honoring thing—that I can do in each situation, and stirs me up to attempt it.

"Paths of Righteousness," 35

REFLECT: My shepherd helps me see and do the most Christlike thing.

Live as free men, but do not use your freedom as a cover-up for evil; live as servants of God.

1 Peter 2:16

Two points that are often overlooked need to be underlined. First, there are many situations in which the general principles of Scripture are all the guidance we either need or get. God often leaves it to us to use the intelligence he gave us in working out the best way to implement biblical principles and priorities. It is part of the process whereby he matures us in Christ. Second, the moral law of Scripture, which is the family code for all God's children, leaves us free to make our own choices as to how we use created things—what interests we pursue, what hobbies we have, and so forth. No guidance is to be expected in these areas beyond the maxims of not letting the good displace the best, not hurting others by the ways in which we enjoy ourselves, and not hurting ourselves by any excessive indulgence that diverts our hearts from heaven to earth and from the Giver to his gifts: in other words, the rules of using liberty responsibly.

"Paths of Righteousness," 35-36

REFLECT: God asks me to use my head, informed by his moral law, as I make decisions.

Do not swerve to the right or the left; keep your foot from evil.
Proverbs 4:27

Balance is the secret of successful tightrope walking. It is also the secret of Christian living. Just as there are always two ways in which a tightrope walker can fall, either to his right or to his left, so it is with the believer. At every point where a policy has to be formed or a course of action planned, two extremes of one-sidedness have to be avoided. But we Christians are abysmally bad at avoiding extremes. We are like pendulums, constantly swinging from one extreme to the other. We see, or think we see, something we dislike and we recoil from it as we would from a snake in the grass. We keep our gaze fixed on it while we put as much distance between it and us as we can. Walking backward in this way, we soon reach an extreme opposite to that which set us going. So one-sidedness of one sort spawns one-sidedness of an opposite sort. Balance is not sought, nor is it found. The reaction of man does not work the righteousness of God.

"Keeping Your Balance: A Christian's Challenge," 18

REFLECT: Without balance, I will avoid one evil only to fall into another.

Be careful to do what the LORD your God has commanded you;
do not turn aside to the right or to the left.

Deuteronomy 5:32

Fifty years ago, evangelicals taught Christian living legalis-
tically: "Don't smoke or drink, cheat, lie, or chew, / And
don't team up with those who do." In those days, avoiding
the world's defilements was the main concern. This school of
thought discounted the idea that Christians are free to enjoy
God's creation while they try to change the world for the
better. Reaction against that thinking has led now to an
opposite extreme. Many Christians have uncritically bought
into the self-indulgent lifestyle of the secular world. Biblical
condemnation of sexual irregularity and the self-serving quest
for wealth, pleasure, and power is ignored, and the behavior
patterns of most Christians seem indistinguishable from those
of unbelievers. In short, ghetto legalism has given way to
antinomian worldliness. Reaction? Yes. Recovery of balance?
No. Disgust at Christian moral laxity will probably soon
spawn a new legalistic rigorism, but that will be reaction
again. Shall we ever achieve Christlike balance and involvement in the world on the basis of being utterly different from
it? At least, for now, let us try!

"Keeping Your Balance: A Christian's Challenge," 18

REFLECT: Both legalism and self-indulgence distort the
gospel.

Show me your ways, O LORD,
teach me your paths;
guide me in your truth and teach me,
for you are God my Savior,
and my hope is in you all day long.

Psalm 25:4-5

We have to be prepared to walk through life with a quiverful of unanswered questions about the ways of God. Why this? Why that? We simply don't know. God doesn't tell us. All that God tells us is how to cope Christianly with this and that as it comes. It's like driving a car. You don't know why people behave on the road in the crazy way they do. But you do know the principles of taking avoiding action and driving correctly amidst strange and bewildering hazards. The Bible guides us in our journey across the rough country of life in just the same way.

It is well to remind ourselves that without biblical truth and wisdom we would be absolutely lost, and to learn to come to Scripture in that healthy frame of mind in which we are very, very conscious of how much we need the light of God to guide us through life's problems. A sense of one's need of God's instruction is the best possible frame of mind for Bible study.

"The Word of Life," 7

REFLECT: I don't need every question answered, but I do need a guide.

Woe to those who call evil good
and good evil,
who put darkness for light
and light for darkness,
who put bitter for sweet
and sweet for bitter.

Isaiah 5:20

What are we to think and do when we find ourselves in situations where we cannot move at all without transgressing a divine prohibition, so that the best we can do is evil from one standpoint? Briefly, love's task then is to find how to do the most good, and the least evil; doing nothing is rarely the answer! Rightly, different principles come out on top in different situations: two Christians armed with "honor your parents" and "do not steal" might well act differently if one Christian could prevent his parents' dying of hunger only by stealing, while the other was being told to steal by his gambling father. But we shall reject the grotesque idea that in such situations law-breaking becomes good; such a valuation leaves no room for regret at having had to do it. Instead, we shall insist that evil remains evil, even when, being the lesser evil, it appears the right thing to do. We shall do it with heavy heart, and seek God's cleansing of our conscience for having done it.

"Situations and Principles," 164

REFLECT: My choices should be directed toward doing the most good and the least evil.

The LORD God commanded the man, "You are free to eat from any tree in the garden; but you must not eat from the tree of the knowledge of good and evil, for when you eat of it you will surely die."

Genesis 2:16-17

God set the first man in a state of happiness and promised to continue this to him and his posterity after him if he showed fidelity by a course of perfect positive obedience, and specifically by not eating from a tree described as the tree of the knowledge of good and evil. It would seem that the tree bore this name because the issue was whether Adam would let God tell him what was good and bad for him or would seek to decide that for himself, in disregard of what God had said. By eating from this tree Adam would, in effect, be claiming that he could know and decide what was good and evil for him without any reference to God.

Concise Theology, 80

REFLECT: God, not man, decides what is good and what is evil.

Grace and peace to you from God our Father and the Lord Jesus Christ, who gave himself for our sins to rescue us from the present evil age, according to the will of our God and Father, to whom be glory for ever and ever. Amen.

Galatians 1:3-5

What does the Bible have to say to our generation, which feels so utterly lost and bedeviled in an inscrutably hostile order of events? There is a plan, says the Bible. There is a sense in circumstances, but you have missed it. Turn to Christ. Seek God. Give yourself to the fulfillment of his plan, and you will have found the elusive key to living. You will have a motive: God's glory. You will have a rule: God's law. You will have a friend in life and death: God's Son. You will have found the answer to the doubting and despair triggered by the apparent meaninglessness, even malice, of circumstances: you will know that the Lord reigns, and that "in all things God works for the good of those who love him, who have been called according to his purpose" (Romans 8:28). And you will have peace.

Hot Tub Religion, 17-18

REFLECT: God has a plan that gives meaning to life.

He who was seated on the throne said, "I am making everything new!" Then he said, "Write this down, for these words are trustworthy and true."

Revelation 21:5

The miracle of God's mercy gives us a new identity, which our self-image must henceforth express. In relation to God, we must see ourselves as *inheritors.* As God's adopted children who will inherit glory, our task for time and eternity is to glorify the One who thus glorifies us. In relation to this life, we must see ourselves as *travelers:* not permanent residents, but pilgrims going home, here to serve but not to settle down. Secular materialism is earthbound, treating this life as all there is, but Christians must look beyond earth (wonderfully good) to heaven (infinitely better), and be ready to let anything go rather than forfeit glory. In relation to worldly pulls, sin's promptings, and satanic prowlings, we must see ourselves as *fighters:* soldiers of Christ who advance by battling opposition with the armor and weapons that Christ supplies. Christians who see themselves in these terms are realists who know who they are, and their new self-image programs them for right living. They are prepared for losses, crosses, changes, and conflicts; they bow low, walk tall, and fight hard all the time.

"Soldier, Son, Pilgrim: Christian Know Thyself," 33

REFLECT: Within God's plan, Christians have a new identity.

This day I call heaven and earth as witnesses against you that I have set before you life and death, blessings and curses. Now choose life, so that you and your children may live.

Deuteronomy 30:19

Free agency is a mark of human beings as such. All humans are free agents in the sense that they make their own decisions as to what they will do, choosing as they please in the light of their sense of right and wrong and the inclinations they feel. Thus they are moral agents, answerable to God and each other for their voluntary choices. So was Adam, both before and after he sinned; so are we now, and so are the glorified saints who are confirmed in grace in such a sense that they no longer have it in them to sin. Inability to sin will be one of the delights and glories of heaven, but it will not terminate anyone's humanness; glorified saints will still make choices in accordance with their nature, and those choices will not be any the less the product of human free agency just because they will always be good and right.

Concise Theology, 85-86

REFLECT: God gives me choice and responsibility.

If anyone chooses to do God's will, he will find out whether my teaching comes from God or whether I speak on my own.

John 7:17

How shall we know what God wants of us? By paying attention to his word and to our own consciences, by noting what circumstances allow, and by taking advice in order to check our own sense of the situation and the adequacy of our insight into what is right. Problems about God's will regularly come clear as they are bounced off other Christian minds. One's own inner state is important too. "If anyone chooses to do God's will," not only will he know that Jesus and his teaching are from God, but he will be told if he is out of the way. "Whether you turn to the right or to the left, your ears will hear a voice behind you, saying, 'This is the way; walk in it'" (Isaiah 30:21). If you are open to God, God will get through to you with the guidance you need. That is a promise!

Growing in Christ, 180-181

REFLECT: While you are unclear as to God's will, wait if you can; if you have to act, make what you think is the best decision, and God will soon let you know if you are not on the right track.

FEBRUARY

God reveals his will
in holy Scripture.

If any of you lacks wisdom, he should ask God, who gives generously to all without finding fault, and it will be given to him. Every good and perfect gift is from above, coming down from the Father of the heavenly lights, who does not change like shifting shadows.

James 1:5, 17

From what source is knowledge of God's work, will, and ways finally and definitively to be drawn? The correct answer, in my view, is: the Bible. It was Wesley who verbalized the practical aim and method of Bible study in the following unforgettable sentences:

"I want to know one thing, the way to heaven.... God himself has condescended to teach the way.... He has written it down in a book. O give me that book: At any price give me the book of God! I have it: here is knowledge enough for me.... I sit down alone: only God is here. In his presence I open, I read his book; for this end, to find the way to heaven.... Does anything appear dark and intricate? I lift up my heart to the Father of Lights.... I then search after and consider parallel passages.... I meditate thereon.... If any doubt still remains, I consult those who are experienced in the things of God: and then the writings whereby, being dead, they yet speak. And what I thus learn, that I teach."

"The Reconstitution of Authority," 10

REFLECT: Bible study helps me understand God's will and God's ways.

"Is not my word like fire," declares the LORD, "and like a hammer that breaks a rock in pieces?"

Jeremiah 23:29

Heaven is not silent; God the Creator has spoken, and the Bible is his written word. God has made himself known on the stage of history by prophecy, by providence, by miracle, and supremely in his Son, Jesus Christ; and Scripture witnesses to that. God has disclosed his will for the living of our lives, and the Bible proclaims his law. God undertakes, through the interpreting work of the Spirit who inspired Scripture in the first place, to teach us how this revelation bears on us; thus it is promised that his word shall function for us as a lamp for our feet and a light to illuminate our path, as on a dark night. God's word is described as a hammer to break stony hearts, fire to burn up rubbish, seed causing birth, milk causing growth, honey that sweetens, and gold that enriches. The Bible is in truth, as the Moderator of the Church of Scotland tells the monarch in the British coronation service, the most precious thing that this world affords.

"Introduction: Why Preach?" 24

REFLECT: Scripture reveals God's will for my life.

We have the word of the prophets made more certain, and you will do well to pay attention to it, as to a light shining in a dark place, until the day dawns and the morning star rises in your hearts.

2 Peter 1:19

What I perceive at the heart of Christianity is God revealing himself in saving love by word and deed within mid-Eastern history, supremely in the incarnation whereby the second person of the Godhead walked and talked as a man among men, but also in the ministry of prophets and apostles and in the Scriptures which are the literary deposit of that ministry; and I perceive the historic Christian tradition, within which I stand and out of which I speak, as a sustained struggle to grasp and apply this uniquely given revelation. So I want to bring this revelation into the present, as best I can, for the light it throws on our perplexities about ourselves, and my hope, as you would expect, is to persuade you to embrace it as the guiding light for your life.

"A Christian View of Man," 103

REFLECT: God's self-revelation in Scripture is my guiding light.

The Mighty One, God, the LORD, speaks and summons the earth from the rising of the sun to the place where it sets.

Psalm 50:1

Yes, God speaks. He condescends to employ human language. The language he gave to his human creatures so that they might talk with each other, he now uses to talk with us. And he also teaches us to use it to respond to him in our praises and prayers. He is thus the God who speaks, just as he is the God who acts. God is not, you see, one who simply speaks and teaches but otherwise does nothing—words without actions—nor is he playing a celestial game of charades—actions without words—on the stage of history, leaving us to guess what the actions mean. Words and deeds belong together in God's self-revelation. God is active in history establishing justice and redeeming sinners, and as he works in power so he speaks by way of narrative and commentary explaining to us what he is doing and why he is doing it.

"The Word of Life," 3

REFLECT: God is not hiding; he says what his actions mean.

Remember your leaders, who spoke the word of God to you. Consider the outcome of their way of life and imitate their faith. Jesus Christ is the same yesterday and today and forever.
Hebrews 13:7-8

God's speaking began in Eden and ended with the apostolic age. Does this mean that for nineteen centuries now God has not been speaking to man at all? No, it does not mean that. It is true that since the apostolic age God has said nothing new to men, for he has in fact no more to say to us than he said then. But it is also true that God has not ceased to say to man all that he said then. The living God is still saying to mankind what he said in and through his Son nineteen centuries ago. Which means that when we read or hear read or expounded the biblical record of what God said in Old or New Testament times, we are as truly confronted by a word of revelation addressed by God to us, and demanding a response from us, as were the Jewish congregations who listened to Jeremiah or Ezekiel or Peter or Christ, or the Gentile congregations who listened to the sermons of the apostle Paul.

God's Words, 23-24

REFLECT: God still speaks through the Bible.

The tablets were the work of God; the writing was the writing of God, engraved on the tablets.

Exodus 32:16

What Scripture says, God says; for, in a manner comparable only to the deeper mystery of the Incarnation, the Bible is both fully human and fully divine. So all its manifold contents—histories, prophecies, poems, songs, wisdom writing, sermons, statistics, letters, and whatever else—should be received as from God, and all that Bible writers teach should be revered as God's authoritative instruction. Christians should be grateful to God for the gift of his written word, and conscientious in basing their faith and life entirely and exclusively upon it. Otherwise, we cannot ever honor or please him as he calls us to do.

Concise Theology, 5

REFLECT: The Bible is God's authoritative word.

What may be known about God is plain to them, because God has made it plain to them. For since the creation of the world God's invisible qualities—his eternal power and divine nature—have been clearly seen, being understood from what has been made.... But their thinking became futile and their foolish hearts were darkened.

Romans 1:19-21

Acceptance of all that Scripture teaches, and refusal either to add to it or subtract from it in our thinking about God, is necessary for two reasons. The first reason is that the fallen human mind, biased and warped as it is by the universal anti-God syndrome called sin, fails to form and own and retain within itself true notions about the Creator drawn from general revelation, whether in the order and course of the world, our own created makeup, or the workings of natural conscience. God's general revelation, though genuinely given to all, is correctly received by none. The second reason is that believers, to whom the Spirit interprets the Scriptures, are nonetheless still prone to lapse intellectually into the world's ways of thinking, just as sometimes they lapse morally into the world's ways of behaving, and so they need constant critical correction and redirection by the word of God.

"Evangelicals and the Way of Salvation," 109

REFLECT: The lens of Scripture helps me interpret this fallen world.

As for you, continue in what you have learned and have become convinced of, because you know those from whom you learned it, and how from infancy you have known the holy Scriptures, which are able to make you wise for salvation through faith in Christ Jesus.

2 Timothy 3:14-15

The Bible is God's letter, consciously addressed by him in his wise providence to every single person who ever reads it. That rather takes one's breath away, doesn't it? But this is the measure of the foreknowledge and wisdom of God: Holy Scripture in its entirety and in each of its parts is the word of God addressed personally to everyone to whom it comes. You have a Bible. Your name is written in the front of the Bible. Think of it as if the Lord himself had written it there. Your Bible is his word addressed to you, and the Lord, in whose presence you read it, wants to know your response to it. It is simply staggering to think of all the millions of Christians there are and have been and will be and to reflect that God in his wisdom has adapted the Bible for the instruction of each one. But that is the truth.

"The Word of Life," 4

REFLECT: My Bible is God's word addressed to me.

They read from the Book of the Law of God, making it clear and giving the meaning so that the people could understand what was being read.

Nehemiah 8:8

Every one of the Bible's sixty-six books, I am bold to say, was written to be understood. Even the more enigmatic ones like Daniel and the visionary parts of Revelation, which seem to us to be written in code, are in fact written in a style that was well understood when these books were first written. Once you and I take the trouble to learn the lingo, our puzzlement will be dispelled. For the rest, however, the Bible doesn't even appear to be written in code. It is written in ordinary, straightforward language with a logical flow, the same sort of language in which we write today for each other's information. We should be listening to hear what the Lord has to say to us in the Bible. As he enables us to see the application, so his word opens our eyes and touches our hearts.

"The Word of Life," 6

REFLECT: The Bible is in itself clear communication from God.

Who among you fears the LORD
and obeys the word of his servant?
Let him who walks in the dark,
who has no light,
trust in the name of the LORD
and rely on his God.

Isaiah 50:10

Holy Scripture is a source of illumination for those who have to take a journey in the dark. Traveling in the dark across rough country, I am at risk. The easiest thing in the world will be for me to stumble and fall over some obstacle I simply can't see. I'm likely to lose the way, miss the path, and get into big trouble. I need a light, a light that will enable me to see the path in front of my feet. God in his mercy has given me such a light. But why, you ask, is the word a lamp and not a sun? Walking by the light of Scripture is not the same as walking by daylight. You can't see everything; in fact, you're often in the dark in every sense and can hardly understand anything of what goes on around you. But Scripture enables you to see each next step you must take, so on you are able to go.

REFLECT: Scripture helps me see my way, one step at a time.

"The Word of Life," 7

Your word is a lamp to my feet
and a light for my path.

Psalm 119:105

See the psalmist's picture. He has to travel. (Scripture regularly pictures life as a journey.) He was in the dark, unable to see the way to go and bound to get lost and hurt if he advanced blindly. (This pictures our natural ignorance of God's will for our lives, our inability to guess it, and the certainty in practice of missing it.) But a lamp (think of a flashlight) has been handed to him. Now he can pick out the path before him, step by step, and stick to it, though darkness still surrounds him. (This pictures what God's word does for us, showing us how to live.) The psalmist's cry is one of *praise* that God glorifies his grace by giving men so precious a gift as his word; *thanks* because he knows how lost he was without it; *admonition* always to value God's word at its true worth; *testimony* to the fact that already in his experience it had proved its power; and *confidence* that this would continue.

God's Words, 39-40

REFLECT: God's word is a light in the darkness.

Humbly accept the word planted in you, which can save you.

James 1:21

God plants the word in our hearts just as we plant bulbs and seeds in our flower pots. The word takes root in our hearts and changes us in ways of which we are not at first conscious; in due course, however, we become aware that we are different from the way we were. Once I didn't see Jesus in his glory, and now I do. Once I didn't love my heavenly Father, and now I do. Once I didn't find worship a joy, and now I do. Once I didn't desire to please God more than I desire anything else in the world; once I didn't desire God's fellowship at all—but that has changed. What has happened? The word has been planted and taken root, and through the Holy Spirit it has become the means of life to my—and your—heart. Bible truth imparts spiritual life, and we need to soak ourselves in Scripture if we are ever to learn how to know and love and serve and honor and obey our Lord.

"The Word of Life," 7-8

REFLECT: When the word is planted in my heart, I change.

Above all, you must understand that no prophecy of Scripture came about by the prophet's own interpretation. For prophecy never had its origin in the will of man, but men spoke from God as they were carried along by the Holy Spirit.

2 Peter 1:20-21

Many today regard Scripture as man's witness to God, and resolve its authority into the authority of the divine words and deeds to which (more or less adequately) witness is borne. But this is only half the truth. Scripture is also, and fundamentally, God's witness to himself, and its authority rests ultimately on the fact that it is his word. Why ought we to believe biblical history, and accept biblical teaching, and confide in Scripture promises, and be governed by Scripture commands? Because Scripture is the written speech of our Creator. "Thus says the *Lord.*" The life of faith and obedience is thus founded on the recognition that what Scripture says, God says. And Christ is not truly Lord in a man's heart till Scripture has been made lord of his mind and conscience. If you would honor Christ and his Father, therefore, bow before Holy Scripture, in which the Father through the Spirit bears witness of his Son. To do this is not superstitious bibliolatry. It is pure and true religion. It is mere Christianity.

God's Words, 37

REFLECT: What Scripture says, God says.

I strive always to keep my conscience clear before God and man.
Acts 24:16

Conscience is the built-in power of our minds to pass moral judgments on ourselves, approving or disapproving our attitudes, actions, reactions, thoughts, and plans, and telling us, if it disapproves of what we have done, that we ought to suffer for it. As distinct from our other powers of mind, conscience is unique: it feels like a person detached from us, often speaking when we would like it to be silent and saying things that we would rather not hear. To the extent that conscience judges us by the highest standard we know, we call it God's voice in the soul. But conscience may be misinformed, or conditioned to regard evil as good, or seared and dulled by repeated sin, and in such cases conscience will be less than God's voice. The particular judgments of conscience are to be received as God's voice only when they match God's own truth and law in Scripture.

Concise Theology, 96-97

REFLECT: My conscience must be educated to judge scripturally.

Dear friends, this is now my second letter to you. I have written both of them as reminders to stimulate you to wholesome thinking. I want you to recall the words spoken in the past by the holy prophets and the command given by our Lord and Savior through your apostles.

2 Peter 3:1-2

We must be clear on the way God speaks to us. What he does is to lead us, whether discursively over a period of time or in a sudden flash of insight (both occur), to see how biblical truth bears on this or that aspect of our own and others' lives. The New Testament directs Christians to get their guidance on faith and life from apostolic teaching backed by the Old Testament—that is, in effect, from the Bible we have—rather than from any nonrational, out-of-the-blue illuminations, and Paul is very hard on the person who rests his faith on visions (see Colossians 2:18). While it is not for us to forbid God to reveal things apart from Scripture, or to do anything else (he is God, after all!), we may properly insist that the New Testament discourages Christians from expecting to receive God's word to them by any other channel than that of attentive application to themselves of what is given to us twentieth-century Christians in Holy Scripture.

God's Words, 39

REFLECT: Scripture is the normal means by which I will learn about God's will and ways.

We know also that the Son of God has come and has given us understanding, so that we may know him who is true. And we are in him who is true—even in his Son Jesus Christ. He is the true God and eternal life.

1 John 5:20

Do you want to know God? Then do as notices at open level crossings tell you to do—stop, look, and listen.

Stop trying to discover God by pursuing thoughts, fancies, and feelings of your own, in disregard of God's revelation. Our knowledge of him and his revelation to us are correlative realities; you do not have the first without the second.

Look at what God has revealed. The Bible is the window through which you may look to see it, and Jesus Christ the Lord, who died and is alive for evermore, is the center of Scripture. Whatever else in the Bible catches your eye, do not let it distract you from him.

Listen to what the Bible tells you about Jesus, and about your need of him. Learn from God about the Son of God; respond to all that you are shown. Do that, and one day you will know revelation from the inside; and in so knowing it you will know God.

God's Words, 28-29

REFLECT: To know God, I must pay attention to his self-revelation.

[Jesus] said to them, "How foolish you are, and how slow of heart to believe all that the prophets have spoken!" And beginning with Moses and all the Prophets, he explained to them what was said in all the Scriptures concerning himself.

Luke 24:25, 27

Too often we approach Holy Scripture simply as a collection of separate stories and sayings, taking for granted that these items represent either moral advice or comfort for those in trouble. God, however, wants us to read the Bible as a *book*—a single story with a single theme. I am not forgetting that the Bible consists of many separate units. For all that, the Bible comes to us as the product of a single mind, the mind of God. It proves its unity over and over again by the amazing way it links together, one part throwing light on another part. So we should read it as a whole, and as we read we are to ask: What is the plot of this book? What is its subject? What is it about? Unless we ask these questions, we will never see what it is saying to us about our lives.

Hot Tub Religion, 11, 13

REFLECT: The Bible is a unity with one author and one story.

These things happened to them as examples and were written down as warnings for us, on whom the fulfillment of the ages has come.

1 Corinthians 10:11

The Bible is as truly a people book as it is a God book, and one of the most interesting and fruitful ways of reading it is to study what it has to say about life. In the Bible you meet all sorts of people, some of them the most vital, virile, forthright, fascinating people you can imagine. And as you read their stories, you learn a great deal about the right way to live and the wrong way to live (or the many wrong ways to live)—both the pitfalls of which life is full and the triumphs in God that those who live rightly may experience. The Bible is focused on people: people to whom God spoke, who either did or did not respond, who obeyed or disobeyed, who found life, who missed life, who entered into spiritual triumph, who experienced spiritual disaster.

"The Word of Life," 3-4

REFLECT: Studying Bible people is a good way to learn how to serve God.

All Scripture is God-breathed and is useful for teaching, rebuking, correcting and training in righteousness.

2 Timothy 3:16

The Bible is overflowing with humanity, full of wisdom about the business of living. There is in fact a whole section called the Wisdom Literature: Psalms, Proverbs, Job, Song of Solomon, and Ecclesiastes in the Old Testament, and James in the New. What seems to me the wisest thing ever said about the five Wisdom books of the Old Testament is this: the Psalms teach you how to pray, Proverbs how to live, Job how to suffer, the Song of Solomon how to love, and Ecclesiastes how to enjoy. That's good philosophy given under God for our learning and our blessing. And then up comes James, the New Testament Wisdom writer, who strikes all these notes together within the compass of his five brief chapters.

"The Word of Life," 4

REFLECT: The Bible is an excellent source of wisdom for daily life.

When he was at the table with them, he took bread, gave thanks, broke it and began to give it to them. Then their eyes were opened and they recognized him, and he disappeared from their sight. They asked each other, "Were not our hearts burning within us while he talked with us on the road and opened the Scriptures to us?"

Luke 24:30-32

The most healing thing in the world to a troubled soul is to find that the heartbreak which produces feelings of isolation, hopelessness, and hatred of all cheerful cackle is actually dealt with in the Bible, and in a way that shows it making sense after all in terms of a loving, divine purpose. And you can be quite certain that the Bible, God's handbook for living, has something to say about every life problem involving God's ways that we shall ever meet. So if you are hurting because of what you feel God has done to you, and you do not find Scripture speaking to your condition, it is not that the Bible now fails you but only that, like these disciples, you do not know it well enough. Ask wiser Christians to open Scripture to you in relation to your pain, and I guarantee that you will find that to be so.

"Walking to Emmaus with the Great Physician," 22-23

REFLECT: The Bible provides comfort for even the deepest pain.

I will instruct you and teach you in the way you should go; I will counsel you and watch over you.

Psalm 32:8

Scripture presents guidance as a covenantal blessing promised to each of God's people in the form of instruction on how to live, both in broad policy terms and in making particular decisions. How does God guide? By instructing. How does he instruct? Partly by his shaping of our circumstances, and partly by his gift of wisdom to understand and digest the teaching of his word and to apply it to ourselves in our circumstances. So God's regular method of guidance is a combination of providential and instructional action. What more he may do in prompting or directing decision in a particular case cannot be anticipated in advance nor made subject of generalization in retrospect. But wisdom will always be given if we are humble and docile enough to receive it.

"Paths of Righteousness," 34

REFLECT: God instructs me by shaping circumstances and by helping me understand and apply his word.

Take the helmet of salvation and the sword of the Spirit, which is the word of God.

Ephesians 6:17

God's teaching in Scripture is our basic guide for living. Bible history and biography illustrate and enforce, both positively and negatively, the divine demand for faith and faithfulness which so many didactic passages spell out. The Holy Spirit who inspired the Scriptures both authenticates them to us as the word of God, making us unable to doubt their authority, and also interprets them to us as we read and meditate on them and hear and read others' expositions of them. Commentaries can tell us what the text meant as an expression of the writer's mind to those to whom he first addressed himself, but only the Holy Spirit can show us what it means as God's word of direction for our life today. Only through the Spirit is guidance from Scripture a reality.

"Paths of Righteousness," 35

REFLECT: The Holy Spirit directs me through the Holy Scriptures.

Do not put out the Spirit's fire; do not treat prophecies with contempt. Test everything. Hold on to the good.

1 Thessalonians 5:19-21

Any direct communications from God will take the form of impressions, and impressions can come even to the most devoted and prayerful people from murky sources, like wishful thinking, fear, obsessional neurosis, schizophrenia, hormonal imbalance, depression, side effects of medication, and satanic delusion, as well as from God. So impressions need to be suspected before they are sanctioned, and tested before they are trusted. Mere confidence that one's impressions are God-given is no guarantee at all that this is really so, even when, as sometimes happens when they are bound up with noble purposes, they persist and grow stronger through long seasons of prayer. To follow impressions, however much they are bound up with the holy concerns of evangelism, intercession, piety, and revival, is not the way to be Spirit-led. Bible-based wisdom must judge them.

"True Guidance," 38

REFLECT: Impressions must be judged by Scripture.

Do not let this Book of the Law depart from your mouth; medi-tate on it day and night, so that you may be careful to do every-thing written in it. Then you will be prosperous and successful.

Joshua 1:8

In our daily pilgrimage, we must learn to listen to God for ourselves. If we dare to ask God to let us hear his word to us personally about our lives, he will. God's word to us is nor-mally heard out of Scripture as it is read, preached, and applied. Soaking our souls in Scripture is our wisdom, there-fore, if we are seeking holiness seriously. A helpful scheme of applicatory meditation on each passage is to ask ourselves:

• What does this passage tell me about God?

• What does this passage tell me about living?

• What does all this say to me about my own life today?

Meditating on these things means thinking them through in the presence of God. Meditation should lead into prayer, in which we talk to God about them directly. This is always the proper conclusion of personal Bible reading.

Rediscovering Holiness, 154-155

REFLECT: Scripture is not only to be read; it is to be savored and applied.

Let the word of Christ dwell in you richly.

Colossians 3:16

Think of your Bible as Jesus Christ's gift to you; think of it as a letter to you from your Lord. Think of your name, written in the front of it, as if Jesus himself had written it there. Think of Jesus each time you read your Bible. Think of him asking you, page by page and chapter by chapter, what you have just learned about the need, nature, method, and effect of the grace that he brings, and about the path of loyal discipleship that he calls you to tread. That is the way to profit from the Bible. Only when your reading of the written word feeds into your relationship with the living Word (Jesus) does the Bible operate as the channel of light and life that God means it to be.

Rediscovering Holiness, 44

REFLECT: The Bible is Christ's personal communication to me.

*Open my eyes that I may see
wonderful things in your law.*

Psalm 119:18

This is a prayer for God to give us insight as we think about his word. God does not mean for Bible reading to function simply as a drug for fretful minds. The reading of Scripture is intended to awaken our minds, not to send them to sleep. God asks us to approach Scripture as his *word*—a message addressed to rational creatures, people with minds; a message we cannot expect to understand without thinking about it. He has taught us to pray for divine enlightenment as we read. But we effectively prevent God from answering this prayer if after praying we blank out and stop thinking.

Hot Tub Religion, 12-13

REFLECT: If I want insight from Scripture, I must be prepared to use my mind.

Train yourself to be godly. For physical training is of some value, but godliness has value for all things, holding promise for both the present life and the life to come.

1 Timothy 4:7-8

A basic dimension of self-training in godliness is learning from the Bible to live by God's truth, and those who do not expend effort in exercising themselves at this point sentence themselves to come short of real godliness at many points. It is ironical to reflect that in a day when the Bible is the world's most widely circulated book, and Christians have more good translations, study Bibles, and other helps to understanding than any previous generation, learning the contents of the Bible is a more neglected discipline than at any time since the Reformation. If we wonder why modern Western churches so conspicuously lack spiritual maturity and are so far from seeing spiritual revival and impacting secular society in a significant way, here is part at least of the answer.

A Passion for Faithfulness, 153-154

REFLECT: A neglected Bible does not train me for godliness.

I will sing to the LORD all my life;
I will sing praise to my God as long as I live.
May my meditation be pleasing to him,
as I rejoice in the LORD.

Psalm 104:33-34

Is there a danger that some people might allow Scripture reading to replace prayer? Yes, if one spends all one's time on simply getting clear the meaning and application of the text, and one doesn't then let one's heart loose in praise and petition in the light of what one now sees. Meditation should naturally lead into praise and prayer. The habit of free, uninhibited praise and thanksgiving across the board of one's life is marvelously enriching. It needs to be a big thing in every Christian's life. The Psalms help a lot in this. Petitions, too, ought to be a regular part of our devotional life. It is assumed in Scripture that we will bring personal petitions and prayer for other people as well. There is something stunted about our spiritual development if we don't.

"Knowing Notions or Knowing God?," 67-68

REFLECT: Scripture study should lead to prayer and praise.

He made known to us the mystery of his will according to his good pleasure, which he purposed in Christ, to be put into effect when the times will have reached their fulfillment—to bring all things in heaven and on earth together under one head, even Christ.

Ephesians 1:9-10

The writers of Scripture saw themselves and their readers as caught up in the outworking of God's sovereign purpose for his world, the purpose that led him to create, that sin then disrupted, and that his work of redemption is currently restoring. That purpose is the endless expression and enjoyment of love between God and his rational creatures. The writers look back at what has already been done to advance God's redemptive plan for sin-damaged earth, and they look ahead to the day when it will be re-created in unimaginable glory. They proclaim God as the almighty Creator-Redeemer and dwell constantly on the multifaceted works of grace that God performs in history to secure for himself a people with whom his original purpose of giving and receiving love can be fulfilled. And the writers insist that as God has shown himself absolutely in control in bringing his plan to the point it has reached as they write, so he will continue in total control, working out everything according to his own will and so completing his redemptive project.

Concise Theology, 37-38

REFLECT: Scripture teaches that God is in control.

MARCH

God wills to rescue us
from sin and death.

I know that nothing good lives in me, that is, in my sinful nature. For I have the desire to do what is good, but I cannot carry it out. For what I do is not the good I want to do; no, the evil I do not want to do—this I keep on doing.

Romans 7:18-19

Paul's cry sums up the question of life's inner contradictions. Why do I so often feel lonely and unfulfilled and impotent and frustrated when I am doing things that I expected to enjoy? Take the matter of relationships. Life, we know, is essentially relationships, and the rich life is the life enriched by one's relationships. But how do enriching relationships happen? How are they achieved? And why do I seem to myself both to want them and not to want them? If close relationships are essential to my fulfillment, why do I shrink from them, as I seem to do? If however they are not essential to my fulfillment, why do I desire them, as again I seem to do?

"A Christian View of Man," 107

REFLECT: I am a human being in contradiction, a problem and a perplexity to myself.

All have sinned and fall short of the glory of God, and are justified freely by his grace through the redemption that came by Christ Jesus.

Romans 3:23-24

Every human individual has infinite worth, being made by God for nobility and glory; but every human individual is currently twisted out of moral shape in a way that only God can cure. To put it in standard Christian language, each of us by nature is God's image-bearer but is also fallen and lives under the power of sin, and now needs grace. Sin, the anti-God allergy of the soul, is a sickness of the spirit; and the tragic sense of life, the inner tensions and contradictions, plus our inveterate unrealism, egoism, and indisposition to love God and our neighbor, are all symptoms of our disorder. In human nature, viewed morally, as God views it, everything is out of true to some extent. And though we have technology for straightening roads and integrating information, it is beyond us to straighten and integrate the human character. Man needs God for that.

"A Christian View of Man," 109

REFLECT: Only God can cure my sin-sickness.

In his pride the wicked does not seek him;
in all his thoughts there is no room for God.

Psalm 10:4

Scripture diagnoses sin as a universal deformity of human nature, found at every point in every person. Both Testaments have names for it that display its ethical character as rebellion against God's rule, missing the mark God set us to aim at, transgressing God's law, disobeying God's directives, offending God's purity by defiling oneself, and incurring guilt before God the Judge. This moral deformity is dynamic: sin stands revealed as an energy of irrational, negative, and rebellious reaction to God's call and command, a spirit of fighting God in order to play God. The root of sin is pride and enmity against God, the spirit seen in Adam's first transgression; and sinful acts always have behind them thoughts, motives, and desires that one way or another express the willful opposition of the fallen heart to God's claims on our lives.

Concise Theology, 82

REFLECT: Sin is putting my will ahead of God's will.

"You will not surely die," the serpent said to the woman. "For God knows that when you eat of it your eyes will be opened, and you will be like God, knowing good and evil."

Genesis 3:4-5

What is the essence of sin? Playing God; and, as a means to this, refusing to allow the Creator to be God so far as you are concerned. Living, not for him, but for yourself; loving and serving and pleasing yourself without reference to the Creator; trying to be as far as possible independent of him, taking yourself out of his hands, holding him at arm's length, keeping the reins of life in your own hands; acting as if you, and your pleasure, were the end to which all things else, God included, must be made to function as a means—that is the attitude in which sin essentially consists. Sin is exalting oneself against the Creator, withholding the homage due to him, and putting oneself in his place as the ultimate standard of reference in all life's decisions.

God's Words, 73

REFLECT: Sin is putting myself in place of my Creator.

Many deceivers, who do not acknowledge Jesus Christ as coming in the flesh, have gone out into the world. Any such person is the deceiver and the antichrist.

2 John 7

Satan's regular way of working is to deceive, and thereby get people to err without any suspicion that what they are thinking and doing is not right. He plays on our pride, will-fulness, unrealism, addictions, stupidities, and temperamental flaws to induce all forms of mental and moral folly—fantasies, cults, idolatries, unbelief, misbelief, dishonesty, infidelity, cru-elty, exploitation, and everything else that degrades and dehumanizes God's image-bearers. Any fancy, feeling, or fashion that works against God and godliness and gives Satan himself room to work as the destroyer of truth, goodness, and beauty in God's world, among God's human creatures, will have full satanic backing. Love, wisdom, humility, and pure-heartedness, four basic components of Christlikeness, are special objects of his attack.

"The Devil's Dossier," 24

REFLECT: Satan is a liar who tricks people into sin.

Encourage one another daily, as long as it is called Today, so that none of you may be hardened by sin's deceitfulness.

Hebrews 3:13

Sin's technique of deception is multiform. Temptation exploits both our temperamental weaknesses and our temperamental strengths. Sin can entangle our minds in a devilish sort of situation ethics whereby we conclude that, whatever might be proper to other situations or for other people, circumstances make what I want to do now all right for me this time. Also, sin can paralyze our minds, so mesmerizing us by the dazzling prospect of what it is open to us to do that reason and conscience cannot get a word in edgeways. (Afterwards we shall say, "I didn't think," and how right we shall be.) Sins of exploiting people, manipulating systems, ducking responsibilities, withholding good will, and working out resentments regularly issue from minds that are entangled; sins of sex, greed, and violence regularly reflect a mind temporarily switched off, a state of affairs to which alcohol, drugs, and exhaustion can contribute disastrously. We need to realize that sin works restlessly within us to produce its horrific effects all the time and that only divine grace can overcome it.

God's Words, 81-82

REFLECT: Sin invades the switched-off mind.

An oracle is within my heart
concerning the sinfulness of the wicked:
There is no fear of God
before his eyes.
For in his own eyes he flatters himself
too much to detect or hate his sin.

Psalm 36:1-2

The deepest division between people in this world may be put as follows: some have knowledge of sin, and some do not. By knowledge of sin I mean an awareness of one's own guilt, perversity, uncleanness and lack of moral and spiritual power as seen by God. Whether such knowledge is ours or not does not depend on whether we live morally or immorally by conventional standards, or whether our chosen lifestyle is orderly and controlled as opposed to wild and random. All that can be said about lifestyle is that if you are *not* one of those who squeeze their living into a mold of conventional respectability so that men will think well of them, you may perhaps be more in touch with yourself and better able to see that the biblical diagnosis of sin is a cap that fits you. In Jesus' day this was true of tax collectors and other disreputables as against the Pharisees, and the pattern has often repeated itself since. Religion can be a role play producing the state of mind which the psalmist ascribes to the wicked.

God's Words, 77-78

REFLECT: My religion leads to wickedness if I do not recognize my own sins.

Everyone who sins breaks the law; in fact, sin is lawlessness.
1 John 3:4

The bad conscience of the natural man is not at all the same thing as conviction of sin. It is not conviction of sin just to feel miserable about yourself and your failures and your inadequacy to meet life's demands. Nor would it be saving faith if a man in that condition called on the Lord Jesus Christ just to soothe him, and cheer him up, and make him feel confident again. We have to go deeper than this. To preach sin means not to make capital out of people's felt frailties but to measure their lives by the holy law of God. To be convicted of sin means to realize that one has offended God, and flouted his authority, and defied him, and gone against him, and put oneself in the wrong with him. To preach Christ means to set him forth as the One who through his cross sets men right with God again. To put faith in Christ means relying on him, and him alone, to restore us to God's fellowship and favor.

Evangelism and the Sovereignty of God, 60-61

REFLECT: Sin goes deeper than failure: it is an offense against God.

Create in me a pure heart, O God,
and renew a steadfast spirit within me.

Psalm 51:10

What are the signs of true conviction of sin, as distinct from the mere smart of a natural bad conscience?

Conviction of sin is essentially an awareness of a wrong relationship with God. It may center upon the sense of one's guilt before God, or one's uncleanness in his sight, or one's estrangement from him, but always it is a sense of the need to get right, not simply with oneself and other people but with one's Maker.

Conviction of sin always includes conviction of *sins:* a sense of guilt for particular wrongs done in the sight of God, from which one needs to turn and be rid of them, if one is ever to be right with God.

Conviction of sin always includes conviction of *sinfulness:* a sense of one's complete corruption and perversity in God's sight and one's consequent need of moral re-creation.

Perhaps the shortest way to tell whether a person is convicted of sin or not is to take him through Psalm 51, and see whether his heart is in fact speaking anything like the language of the psalmist.

Evangelism and the Sovereignty of God, 62-63

REFLECT: Sin is a broken relationship with God.

It is impossible for those who have once been enlightened, who have tasted the heavenly gift, who have shared in the Holy Spirit, who have tasted the goodness of the word of God and the powers of the coming age, if they fall away, to be brought back to repentance, because to their loss they are crucifying the Son of God all over again and subjecting him to public disgrace.

Hebrews 6:4-6

It is possible for people to be enlightened to the point of knowing inwardly that Jesus is the divine Savior he claims to be, and still not be willing to admit it publicly, because of all the behavioral changes that such an admission would make necessary. It is possible to try to make oneself feel good about one's own moral dishonesty by inventing reasons, no matter how absurd, for not treating Jesus as worthy of one's allegiance. This hardening of heart against Jesus would preclude any remorse at any stage for having thus blasphemed. But nonexistence of remorse makes repentance impossible, and nonexistence of repentance makes forgiveness impossible. Callousing one's conscience by dishonest reasonings so as to justify denial of God's power in Christ and rejection of his claims upon one is, then, the formula of the unpardonable sin. But Christians who fear that they may have committed the unpardonable sin show by their very anxiety that they have not done so. Persons who have committed it are unremorseful and unconcerned; indeed, they are ordinarily unaware of what they have done and to what fate they have sentenced themselves.

Concise Theology, 244-246

REFLECT: The only unpardonable sin is the unrepented sin.

God demonstrates his own love for us in this: While we were still sinners, Christ died for us.

Romans 5:8

The gospel announces God's love to all of us sinners and teaches us to measure it by setting three things together: how guilty and nasty our holy Creator sees us to be; how far he went to save us, giving his Son to taste the hell we deserved in order to secure our rescue; and the reality of full forgiveness, acceptance, restoration to fellowship and a clean slate, as God's free gift through Christ to penitent believers. The gospel takes us lower in self-abhorrence and despair than inferiority feelings ever do, and raises us to an awestruck joy that those with a "good" self-image never reach. From this a changed view of ourselves must result. However unloved and worthless we once felt, we must now see that by loving us enough to redeem us God gave us value, and by forgiving us completely he obligated us to forgive ourselves. So the old way of thinking and feeling about ourselves must be driven out by a new one, which is to last for the rest of our lives.

"Soldier, Son, Pilgrim: Christian Know Thyself," 33

REFLECT: The gospel reveals God's love for sinners.

When Jesus spoke again to the people, he said, "I am the light of the world. Whoever follows me will never walk in darkness, but will have the light of life."

John 8:12

What does God say in the gospel—that is, the good news (which is what "gospel" means) concerning God's love to the lost? He announces the most staggering free gift of all time. He offers total rescue (that is, *salvation*) from the rebellious nonconformity to himself which is the root of all our guilt, misery, and frustration, and whose Bible name is *sin*. He promises a new, endless life of pardon, peace, moral power, and joyful purpose to all who are humble enough not to try and earn it, but simply to receive it. How can God make this offer? Through Christ's death as a sacrifice for sins. How do we receive this life? By renouncing rebellion and embracing the risen Savior as our Master; the life is found within that relationship. What happens then? Increasingly we prove the truth of Jesus' words, "Whoever follows me... will have the light of life."

Growing in Christ, 104

REFLECT: The gospel announces God's gift of new life.

I delight greatly in the LORD;
my soul rejoices in my God.
For he has clothed me with garments of salvation.

Isaiah 61:10

The master theme of the Christian gospel is salvation. *Salvation* is a picture word of wide application that expresses the idea of rescue from jeopardy and misery into a state of safety. What are believers saved *from?* From their former position under the wrath of God, the dominion of sin, and the power of death; from their natural condition of being mastered by the world, the flesh, and the devil; from the fears that a sinful life engenders, and from the many vicious habits that were part of it. What are they saved *for?* To live for time and eternity in love to God—Father, Son, and Spirit—and to their neighbors. God's purpose, here and hereafter, is to keep expressing his love in Christ to us, and our goal must be to keep expressing our love to the three Persons of the one God by worship and service in Christ. The life of love and adoration is our hope of glory, our salvation now, and our happiness forever.

Concise Theology, 146-148

REFLECT: God has saved me *from* sin and *for* love.

Christ's love compels us, because we are convinced that one died for all, and therefore all died. And he died for all, that those who live should no longer live for themselves but for him who died for them and was raised again.

2 Corinthians 5:14-15

It is often and truly said that the gospel message, through the power of the Spirit of Christ that it mediates, turns people's lives upside down. Less frequently it is noted that the anti-God syndrome in our system called original sin had turned our lives upside down already, so that this inverting change of heart by the Spirit, commonly called conversion, actually sets us right way up, to live in the way truly natural to us for the first time ever. In a sovereign act of grace God unites the individual to the risen Lord in such a way that the dispositional drives of Christ's perfect human character—the inner urgings, that is, to honor, adore, love, obey, serve, and please God, and to benefit others for both their sake and his sake—are now reproduced at the motivational center of that individual's being.

"Evangelicals and the Way of Salvation," 152

REFLECT: The gospel of Christ turns me right side out.

If we confess our sins, he is faithful and just and will forgive us our sins and purify us from all unrighteousness.

1 John 1:9

Forgiveness is pardon in a personal setting. It is taking back into friendship those who went against you, hurt you, and put themselves in the wrong with you. It is compassionate (showing unmerited kindness to the wrongdoer), creative (renewing the spoiled relationship)—and, inevitably, costly. God's forgiveness is the supreme instance of this, for it is God in love restoring fellowship at the cost of the cross. Is God's gift of forgiveness by faith yours yet? It is easily missed. The pathetic truth is that we sinners are self-righteous to the core, and we are constantly justifying ourselves. We hate admitting that there is anything seriously wrong with us, anything that God or man might seriously hold against us; and we have to do violence to our own perverted instincts at this point before faith is possible for us.

Growing in Christ, 80-82

REFLECT: God is ready to forgive me, if I am ready to confess that I need forgiveness.

He saved us through the washing of rebirth and renewal by the Holy Spirit, whom he poured out on us generously through Jesus Christ our Savior, so that, having been justified by his grace, we might become heirs having the hope of eternal life.

Titus 3:5-7

Jesus' prescription of baptism for all disciples (Matthew 28:19) shows us that we all need heavenly washing. This washing is momentous. It includes both the canceling of guilt by pardon and the breaking of sin's dominion—that is, our enslavement to motives which, by exalting and indulging self, defile and pollute our whole lives. When are we thus washed? When we believe—that is, commit ourselves to Christ. What then has baptism to do with it? Three things. First, baptism symbolically *pictures* it, for our learning. Second, baptism visibly *promises* it, proclaiming that whoever has faith in Christ will receive it. Third, baptism formally *presents* it, and so assures the believing recipient that he really has it. Are you washed? Like me, you need to be.

Growing in Christ, 116-117

REFLECT: Baptism shows that my sins have been forgiven and washed away.

Forgive us our sins, for we also forgive everyone who sins against us.

Luke 11:4

Christians must be willing to examine themselves and let others examine them for the detecting of day-to-day short-comings. The Puritans valued preachers who would "rip up" the conscience; more such preaching is needed today. The discipline of self-examination, though distasteful to our pride, is necessary because our holy Father in heaven will not turn a blind eye to his children's failings, as human parents so often (and so unwisely) do. What he knows about our sins we need to know too, so that we may repent and ask pardon for whatever has given offense. The communion service in the 1662 Prayer Book teaches Christians to call the "burden" (guilt) of their sins "intolerable." The justification for this strong language is knowledge of the intolerable grief brought to God by the sins of his own family. The true Christian will not only seek to find and face his sins through self-examination, but he will labor "by the Spirit" to "put to death the misdeeds of the body" (that is, the habits of the old sinful self) all his days.

Growing in Christ, 192-193, 216-217

REFLECT: Regular self-examination is vital to the Christian life.

Those who oppose him he must gently instruct, in the hope that God will grant them repentance leading them to a knowledge of the truth, and that they will come to their senses and escape from the trap of the devil, who has taken them captive to do his will.

2 Timothy 2:25-26

Repentance is a change of mind issuing in a change of life. Since practical atheism, which disregards God, is natural to fallen human beings, godliness has to be founded on repentance from the start. Repentance means a right-face turn and a quick march in the direction opposite to that in which we were going before. The original direction was the path of self-service, in the sense of treating yourself as God, the supreme value, and gratifying yourself accordingly. The new direction is a matter of saying good-bye to all that and embracing the service of God instead. The fact we must face is that impenitent and unconsecrated Christians will be out of earshot when God calls them to service. Apathy and sluggishness with regard to ordinary obedience brings deafness when God calls to special service.

A Passion for Faithfulness, 58

REFLECT: Repentance precedes service.

Have mercy on me, O God,
according to your unfailing love;
according to your great compassion
blot out my transgressions.

Psalm 51:1

Christians are called to a life of habitual repentance, as a discipline integral to healthy holy living.

In my part of British Columbia, where rainfall is heavy, roads on which the drains fail soon get flooded and become unserviceable. Repentance is the draining routine on the highway of holiness on which God calls us all to travel. It is the way we get beyond what has proved to be dirt, rubbish, and stagnant flood water in our lives. This routine is a vital need, for where real repentance fails, real spiritual advance ceases, and real spiritual growth stops short.

It is the wisdom of churches that use liturgies to provide prayers of penitence for use at all services. Such prayers are always words in season. In our private devotions, daily penitential prayer will always be needed too.

Rediscovering Holiness, 122

REFLECT: Repentance should be a habit.

Let us examine our ways and test them, and let us return to the LORD.

Lamentations 3:40

I believe that even as we who are Christians ought to praise God, give him thanks, and make requests to him daily, so we ought to repent daily. This discipline is as basic to holiness as any. Whatever else was wrong with the old practice of penance, its requirement of regular reporting in the confessional at least kept believers aware that facing, forsaking, and fighting sin is a constant task. The further one goes in holy living, the more sin one will find in the attitudes of one's own heart, needing to be dealt with in this way. As the single-mindedness of our inward devotion is the real index of the quality of our discipleship, so the thoroughness of our daily repentance is the real index of the quality of our devotion. There is no way around that.

Rediscovering Holiness, 144

REFLECT: Repentance should be daily—and thorough.

Wash away all my iniquity
and cleanse me from my sin.
For I know my transgressions,
and my sin is always before me.

Psalm 51:2-3

Godly Christians have always been marked by a two-sided perception of divine holiness. On the one hand, the transcendent glory of God's purity and love, as focused in the plan of salvation, fascinates them. On the other hand, the transcendent glory of God's sovereignty, as focused in the divine threat of judgment for impiety, alarms them. This characteristically Christian sense of the mercy and the terror (fear) of the Lord is the seedbed in which awareness grows that lifelong repentance is a "must" of holy living. That awareness will not grow under any other conditions. Where it is lacking, any supposed sanctity will prove on inspection to be flawed by complacency about oneself and shortsightedness about sin. Show me, then, a professed Christian who does not see and insist on the need for ongoing repentance, and I will show you a stunted soul for whom God is not as yet the Holy One in the full biblical sense.

Rediscovering Holiness, 132

REFLECT: I will need to continue repenting for as long as I live.

Search me, O God, and know my heart;
test me and know my anxious thoughts.
See if there is any offensive way in me,
and lead me in the way everlasting.

Psalm 139:23-24

Those who neglect the discipline of thorough repentance for their shortcomings, along with regular self-examination so as to discern those shortcomings, are behaving as if God just turns a blind eye to our moral flaws. But God is not morally indifferent, and we must not act toward him as if he were. The only way to show real respect for God's real purity is by realistically setting oneself against sin. That means repentance—not mere routine words of regret as one asks for pardon without one's heart being involved, but a deliberate confessing, an explicit self-humbling, and a sensing of shame in the presence of God as one contemplates one's failures. For God's purity leads him to hate evil. His demand that we be like him requires us to become haters of it too, starting with the evil that we find inside ourselves.

Rediscovering Holiness, 145-146

REFLECT: It is right to feel shame and guilt when I find evil in my life.

Surely you desire truth in the inner parts;
you teach me wisdom in the inmost place.
Cleanse me with hyssop, and I will be clean;
wash me, and I will be whiter than snow.

Psalm 51:6-7

In their dreams and desires, even if not in their outward behavior, Christians too have their lapses into coveting, lusting, greed, malice, and deceitfulness. Christians, like others, are tempted to be self-indulgent, to abuse and exploit their fellow human beings, to treat might as right in the realm of relationships, and on occasion to wish others dead. Whether or not God in his providence keeps us from acting these things out is not the issue. The point is that the disordered desires were there, and when our hearts embraced them, our hearts were wrong. That is what we need to repent of.

Rediscovering Holiness, 149

REFLECT: I need to repent of disordered desires as well as disorderly behavior.

If your hand or your foot causes you to sin cut it off and throw it away. It is better for you to enter life maimed or crippled than to have two hands or two feet and be thrown into eternal fire.

Matthew 18:8

While surrendering sins into which you drifted casually is not so hard, mortifying what the Puritans called "besetting" sins—dispositional sins to which your temperament inclines you, and habitual sins that have become addictive and defiant—is regularly a long-drawn-out, bruising struggle. No one who is a spiritual realist will ever pretend otherwise. It is a matter of negating, wishing dead, and laboring to thwart inclinations, cravings, and habits that have been in you for a long time. Pain and grief, moans and groans, will certainly be involved, for your sin does not want to die, nor will it enjoy the killing process. Jesus told us, very vividly, that mortifying a sin could well feel like plucking out an eye or cutting off a hand or foot, in other words, self-mutilation. You will feel you are saying good-bye to something that is so much part of you that without it you cannot live.

Rediscovering Holiness, 175

REFLECT: Mortifying sin, however painful, is a necessity for life in Christ.

They refused to listen and failed to remember the miracles you performed among them.... But you are a forgiving God, gracious and compassionate, slow to anger and abounding in love. Therefore you did not desert them.

Nehemiah 9:17

The Christian under grace is freed from the hopeless necessity of trying to commend himself to God by perfect law-keeping. Now he lives by being forgiven, and so is free at every point in his life to fail (as inevitably he does in fact, again and again)—and, having failed, to pick himself up where he fell, to seek and find God's pardon, and to start again. Pride, our natural disposition, which is self-protective, self-righteous, and vainglorious, will either refuse to admit failure at all or refuse to try again, lest the trauma of failing be repeated; but the humility of the man who lives by being forgiven knows no such inhibitions. Daily the Christian's shortcomings are forgiven and his joy restored. One reason why, as Jesus taught, we must be ready to forgive our fellow Christians countless times is that our own life with God is a matter of being forgiven countless times, too.

God's Words, 106

REFLECT: I live by daily forgiveness.

Remember how the LORD your God led you all the way in the desert these forty years, to humble you and to test you in order to know what was in your heart, whether or not you would keep his commands.

Deuteronomy 8:2

Scripture speaks of both God and Satan testing (or "tempting")—that is, trying people out to see what is in them. We read that Jesus was tempted by the devil (Matthew 4:1) and that God tested Abraham (Genesis 22:1), and the truth is that in every testing situation both Satan and God are involved. God tests us to bring forth excellence in discipleship. Satan, by contrast, tests us with a view to our ruin and destruction. Temptation is always two-sided in this way; so whenever we are conscious of Satan seeking to pull us down, we should remind ourselves that God is present too to keep us steady and to build us up through the harrowing experience. That is something we must never forget.

A Passion for Faithfulness, 114-115

REFLECT: Whenever Satan tempts me, God is there to keep me from falling.

If you live according to the sinful nature, you will die; but if by the Spirit you put to death the misdeeds of the body, you will live.
Romans 8:13

How do we "by the Spirit ... put to death the misdeeds of the body"? Outward acts of sin come from inner sinful urges, so we must learn to starve these urges of what stimulates them (porn magazines, for instance, if the urge is lust; visits to smorgasbords, if the urge is gluttony; gambling and lotteries, if the urge is greed; and so on). And when the urge is upon us, we must learn, as it were, to run to our Lord and cry for help, asking him to deepen our sense of his own holy presence and redeeming love, to give us the strength to say no to that which can only displease him. It is the Spirit who moves us to act this way, who makes our sense of the holy love of Christ vivid, who imparts the strength for which we pray, and who actually drains the life out of the sins we starve.

Rediscovering Holiness, 175

REFLECT: The Holy Spirit helps me starve my sinful urges.

If, when we were God's enemies, we were reconciled to him through the death of his Son, how much more, having been reconciled, shall we be saved through his life! Not only is this so, but we also rejoice in God through our Lord Jesus Christ, through whom we have now received reconciliation.

Romans 5:10-11

God draws us into fellowship with himself by different routes; it is a mistake to expect one person's journey into faith to be a carbon copy of another's. The demand that conversion experiences correspond only stirs up misplaced and distracting anxieties. We are all different people with different starting points, and God deals with us as we are where he finds us. Richard Baxter said, "God breaketh not all men's hearts alike." But at one point all the roads to Christ converge: at the point of realizing that one is out of step and out of fellowship with God, and has no hope but in the reconciliation that Christ himself brings. Real Christianity—the life of knowing God, as distinct from the life of being prepared for knowing God—starts here, in what Paul calls the receiving of reconciliation; here, and nowhere else.

God's Words, 127

REFLECT: God takes me where he finds me and brings me to himself.

I always thank God for you because of his grace given you in Christ Jesus.

1 Corinthians 1:4

You give God thanks for your conversion. Why? Because you know in your heart that God was entirely responsible for it. You did not save yourself; he saved you. You do not put it down to chance or accident that you came under Christian influence when you did—that you attended a Christian church, heard the Christian gospel, had Christian friends and perhaps a Christian home, saw your need of Christ and came to trust him as your Savior. You do not attribute your repenting and believing to your own wisdom, or prudence, or sound judgment, or good sense. Your act of faith when you closed with Christ was yours in the sense that it was you who performed it; but that does not mean that you saved yourself. You give God all the glory for all that your salvation involved, and you know that it would be blasphemy if you refused to thank him for bringing you to faith. Thus you acknowledge the sovereignty of divine grace. And every other Christian in the world does the same.

Evangelism and the Sovereignty of God, 12-13

REFLECT: Conversion is a response to God's grace.

Praise be to the God and Father of our Lord Jesus Christ,... for he chose us in him before the creation of the world to be holy and blameless in his sight.

Ephesians 1:3-4

The hearts of saved people will always affirm that their conversion, or new birth, or renewal (different people use different words) was the work of God from first to last. All the searching and struggling that went into it will be felt to have been no less divinely orchestrated than were its final stages of conviction, commitment, and assurance. The sense that God has thus invaded one's own darkness and lostness in order to bring salvation naturally prompts the question that was poignantly posed in a modern gospel song—"But, Jesus, why me?" The New Testament faces and answers this question by pointing backward and upward to an eternal purpose of sovereign divine love to sinful individuals, a purpose that has its source in God's own free decision. New Testament writers do not tell me why God chose to save me. They only tell me to be thankful that he did.

Rediscovering Holiness, 55-56

REFLECT: Amazing grace—God has chosen to save me!

I am the least of the apostles and do not even deserve to be called an apostle, because I persecuted the church of God. But by the grace of God I am what I am, and his grace to me was not without effect.

1 Corinthians 15:9-10

To the New Testament writers, grace is a wonder. Their sense of man's corruption and demerit before God, and of the reality and justice of his wrath against sin, is so strong that they find it simply staggering that there should be such a thing as grace at all—let alone grace that was so costly to God as the grace of Calvary. The hymn writers catch this sense of wonder with their use of "amazed" and "amazing" in such lines as "Amazing love! how can it be that thou, my God, shouldst die for me?"; "Love so amazing, so divine, demands my soul, my life, my all"; "I stand all amazed at the love Jesus offers me"; "Amazing grace!" The world is full of wonders—wonders of nature, wonders of science, wonders of craftsmanship—but they pale into insignificance beside the wonder of the grace of God. Nothing we say can do it justice: all words fall short of it: it is, in truth, as Paul says, an "indescribable gift!" (2 Corinthians 9:15).

God's Words, 98-99

REFLECT: God's grace is a wonder that is beyond human understanding.

APRIL

God unites us in community
to do his will.

Husbands, love your wives, just as Christ loved the church and gave himself up for her to make her holy, cleansing her by the washing with water through the word, and to present her to himself as a radiant church, without stain or wrinkle or any other blemish, but holy and blameless.

Ephesians 5:25-27

He was an odd little man, lean, intense, and jerky, with a face that seemed to light up as he spoke. I was there out of loyalty to the college chapel, not expecting to be impressed; but he captured my attention telling us how in his teens he had experienced a personal conversion to Jesus Christ, like that which I had just undergone myself. "And then," he said, "I got excited about the church. You could say, I fell in love with it." He then hammered home the point that all who love Jesus Christ the Lord ought to care deeply about the church, because the church is the object of Jesus' own love. Church-centeredness is thus one way in which Christ-centeredness ought to find expression. Was he right? Yes, he was: no question about that. Something is wrong with professed Christians who do not identify with the church, and love it, and invest themselves in it, and carry its needs on their hearts.

A Passion for Faithfulness, xii-xiii

REFLECT: The church is the object of Jesus' love.

Praise be to the Lord, the God of Israel, because he has come and has redeemed his people. He has raised up a horn of salvation for us in the house of his servant David (as he said through his holy prophets of long ago),... to show mercy to our fathers and to remember his holy covenant.

Luke 1:68-70, 72

Christ's church was to be, and now is, the Old Testament covenant community itself in a new and fulfilled form that God had planned for it from the start. It is Israel internationalized and globally extended in, through, and under the unifying dominion of Jesus, the divine Savior who is its King. It is God the Father's family, as appears from the fact that Jesus taught his followers to think and speak of his heavenly Father as theirs too. It is the risen Christ's body and bride, destined for the ultimate in intimacy with him and the sharing of his life. It is the fellowship of the Holy Spirit, the unseen but potent divine facilitator who shows us that Jesus the Christ is real today, who sustains our trust in him and our love for him, who shapes and reconstructs our character in his likeness, and who supplies us with abilities for mutual ministry. In a word, the church is the community that lives in and by covenant communion between the triune God and itself.

A Passion for Faithfulness, xvi

REFLECT: The church is the covenant community of fellowship between God and man.

[God] says to Moses, "I will have mercy on whom I have mercy, and I will have compassion on whom I have compassion." It does not, therefore, depend on man's desire or effort, but on God's mercy.

Romans 9:15-16

The biblical doctrine of election is that before creation God selected out of the human race, foreseen as fallen, those whom he would redeem, bring to faith, justify, and glorify in and through Jesus Christ. The doctrine of election, like every truth about God, involves mystery and sometimes stirs controversy. But in Scripture it is a pastoral doctrine, brought in to help Christians see how great is the grace that saves them, and to move them to humility, confidence, joy, praise, faithfulness, and holiness in response. It is the family secret of the children of God. We do not know who else he has chosen among those who do not yet believe, nor why it was his good pleasure to choose us in particular. What we do know is, first, that had we not been chosen for life we would not be believers now (for only the elect are brought to faith), and, second, that as elect believers we may rely on God to finish in us the good work that he started.

Concise Theology, 149-150

REFLECT: Knowledge of my election in Christ brings comfort and joy.

Be devoted to one another in brotherly love. Honor one another above yourselves.

Romans 12:10

As the church consists of individuals who, by coming to faith and associating as believers, have become the Lord's people, so Christ's building of the church is a matter of his so changing people on the inside—in their hearts, as we say—that repentance, faith, and obedience become more and more the pattern of their lives. Thus increasingly they exhibit the humility, purity, love, and zeal for God that we see in Jesus, and fulfill Jesus' call to worship, work, and witness in his name. And this they do, not as isolated individuals (lone-rangerism!), but as fellow siblings in God's family, helping and encouraging each other in the openness and mutual care that are the hallmarks of "brotherly love." Hereby they enter increasingly into the life that constitutes authentic Christianity, the life of fellowship with their heavenly Father, their risen Savior, and each other.

A Passion for Faithfulness, xvii-xviii

REFLECT: Authentic Christianity is a life of fellowship.

Now I commit you to God and to the word of his grace, which can build you up and give you an inheritance among all those who are sanctified.

Acts 20:32

"Build up" is the same word as in Matthew 16:18, "On this rock I will build my church," and here too, as indeed throughout the New Testament, it has a corporate frame of reference. The building up of individuals is the winding down of individualism, for it is precisely the building of them into the communal network called the church. The word, ministered, memorized, and masticated by meditation, has power to do the building up through the agency of the Holy Spirit. And within the church on earth this process of building up—or building in, as we might equally well call it when we focus on the people who are its object—goes on all the time. Jesus builds his church, according to his word.

A Passion for Faithfulness, xx-xxi

REFLECT: Jesus builds his people into his church.

I confess the sins we Israelites, including myself and my father's house, have committed against you. We have acted very wickedly toward you. We have not obeyed the commands, decrees and laws you gave your servant Moses.

Nehemiah 1:6-7

In this plea Nehemiah's expression of solidarity with the Jerusalem Jews is unqualified and complete. He acknowledges solidarity because he knows that is how God sees it. So he accepts a share in the shame of the people now under judgment, and in this he is a model for us. Solidarity as communal involvement according to the Scriptures—the solidarity of the family, the nation, and the church—is something that we today do not understand very well. Western culture teaches us to treat ourselves as isolated individuals and to excuse ourselves from accepting solidarity with any group, especially when the solidarity is one of disrepute. Nehemiah, however, knew that God saw the Jews as one family with a corporate responsibility and a corporate destiny, and unhesitatingly identified with them in the guilt that had brought them under judgment.

A Passion for Faithfulness, 47

REFLECT: I am not alone: my life is tied up with the life of my family, community, and church.

I am the good shepherd. The good shepherd lays down his life for the sheep.

John 10:11

By acknowledging Jesus as our shepherd we affirm identification with his flock—the community for which "Jesus people" is the perfect name, the Christian church. They are our compatriots, fellow nationals, for "our citizenship is in heaven" (Philippians 3:20); they are our brothers and sisters, with us in God's family, for "you are all brothers" (Matthew 23:8); and they are limbs with us in the ministering organism which is Christ's body, "for we are all members of one body" (Ephesians 4:25). So baptism has social implications. Involvement in the "body life" of mutual sympathy and service for Christ must be the rule for all the baptized. Isolationism in church—sitting apart, not getting acquainted, dodging responsibility, and so on—denies the meaning of baptism.

Growing in Christ, 112-113

REFLECT: Baptized Christians are members together of Christ's body.

Some men came down from Judea to Antioch and were teaching the brothers: "Unless you are circumcised,... you cannot be saved." This brought Paul and Barnabas into sharp dispute and debate with them. So Paul and Barnabas were appointed, along with some other believers, to go up to Jerusalem to see the apostles and elders about this question.

Acts 15:1-2

We were neither made nor redeemed for self-sufficient aloneness, and it is not to be expected that our private stock of wisdom and discernment will suffice without supplement from outside sources. We must never be too proud to take advice from persons wiser and godlier than ourselves, and any personal guidance that we think we have received by inner nudge from the Lord ought to be checked with believers who are capable of recognizing unrealism, delusion, and folly when they see it. In these two ways the Spirit regularly uses the fellowship of the body of Christ to deepen each Christian's discernment of God's will, and it is part of the discipline of divine guidance to be ready for the Spirit to speak to us through other believers to confirm his will for our lives.

"Paths of Righteousness," 37

REFLECT: The Spirit speaks to me through the wisdom of other believers.

Confess your sins to each other and pray for each other so that you may be healed. The prayer of a righteous man is powerful and effective.

James 5:16

James is talking of the intimacies of Christian friendship in what are nowadays called "accountability relationships." In accountability relationships, one cares for another in a context of open sharing of lives: sad things like failures and falls, as well as glad things like deliverances and successes. Confession of sins within friendships of this kind is an important expression of repentance. Embarrassment should not be allowed to hold us back.

To confess one's sins to a peer and a friend is to commit oneself to redoubled effort not to lapse that way again. To ask one's friend to pray that one may be healed is to make oneself accountable for maintaining that commitment on a permanent basis. Few of us, I think, really know the value of accountability relationships in the battle for honest repentance and for wholeheartedness in fighting temptations to sin.

Rediscovering Holiness, 142

REFLECT: I need Christian friends to pray for me and hold me accountable in my battle with sin.

If your brother sins against you, go and show him his fault, just between the two of you. If he listens to you, you have won your brother over. But if he will not listen, take one or two others along, so that "every matter may be established by the testimony of two or three witnesses."

Matthew 18:15-16

There are good and bad ways of fulfilling the ministry of criticism among Christians. This ministry is important, for all we who seek truth and wisdom take up from time to time with wrong ideas and need correction. But discussion and debate ordinarily achieve more than gestures of denunciation. To think of sustained denunciation as the essence of faithful witness, and of the mindset that will not see any good in what is not totally good as a Christian virtue, is very wrong. Denouncing error has its place, but since it easily appears arrogant and generates much unfruitful unhappiness, anyone who feels drawn to it should take a lot of advice before yielding to the urge.

"Packer the Picketed Pariah," 11

REFLECT: Criticism is an important but dangerous ministry.

I urge you to live a life worthy of the calling you have received. Be completely humble and gentle; be patient, bearing with one another in love. Make every effort to keep the unity of the Spirit through the bond of peace.

Ephesians 4:1-3

The gospel fosters *individuality*, in the sense of realization that as regards the present decisions that determine eternal destiny one stands alone before God; no one can make those decisions for someone else. The individuality that consists of a sense of personal identity and responsibility Godward is a Christian virtue, making for wise and thoughtful behavior, and is a necessity for mature life and growth in Christ. But it has nothing to do with *individualism*, which is actually a proud unwillingness to accept a place in a team of peers and to be bound by group consensus. The gospel condemns individualism as disruptive of the life of the divine family, the new community of believers together that God is building in each place where individual Christians have emerged. Harmonious consensus, undergirded by brotherly love, is to be the goal for every church, and individualism is to be overcome by mutual deference.

"Evangelicals and the Way of Salvation," 160

REFLECT: Christians care for one another.

They devoted themselves to the apostles' teaching and to the fellowship, to the breaking of bread and to prayer.

Acts 2:42

What are the means of growth, the means whereby this work of God is carried on in your life and mine? Theological textbooks speak of "the means of grace," which are usually listed something like this: *Bible truth,* preached and received through preaching, studied in the text, meditated on, applied to oneself, taken to heart, laid up in the memory, taken as a guide for life; *prayer,* the regular exercise of communion and fellowship with God; *worship* with the Lord's people, particularly at the Lord's Supper but also in hearing the word regularly proclaimed and joining in the prayers and the vocal praise; and the *informal fellowship* and interchange of the Lord's family as one stands by and ministers to another.

"The Means of Growth," 10

REFLECT: God wants me to use the means he has provided to grow in his grace.

The grace of God that brings salvation has appeared to all men. It teaches us to say "No" to ungodliness and worldly passions, and to live self-controlled, upright and godly lives in this present age.

Titus 2:11-12

The church is the body of Christ, called under the leadership of Jesus, its head, to permeate and purify society and inject God's values, which are the true human values, into its life. But Satan's empire (that is, pagan and secular ideologies and the communities that embrace them) strikes back. The New Testament writers regularly speak of the world in a human and cultural sense, meaning society organized apart from God and against God, and they see the world as always trying to squeeze Christians individually and the church corporately into its own mold—the mold, that is, of the predominant preconceptions, prejudices, behavior patterns, and styles of life of the particular time and place in which God's people find themselves. The conflict is continuous.

A Passion for Faithfulness, 178

REFLECT: The church and the world are in constant conflict.

Depart, depart, go out from there!
Touch no unclean thing!
Come out from it and be pure,
you who carry the vessels of the LORD.

Isaiah 52:11

Of the church in the world it has been said that while the place for the ship is in the sea, it can only mean disaster when the sea gets into the ship, and this is the truth. Sub-Christian bilge is always seeping into the church and needs to be pumped out; sometimes, too, a battening down of hatchways is needed to prevent the vessel's being swamped by this or that inundation. When God's people cease to be on watch against the world, they are already in its grip, and continuous weakening is all that can be expected as long as this negligence lasts. Meantime, worldly-mindedness, thus induced, will be leading to broken vows and broken lives.

A Passion for Faithfulness, 178-179

REFLECT: Christians are called to be separated to God and therefore different from others in their way of life.

People will be lovers of themselves, lovers of money, boastful, proud, abusive, disobedient to their parents, ungrateful, unholy, without love, unforgiving, slanderous, without self-control, brutal, not lovers of the good, treacherous, rash, conceited, lovers of pleasure rather than lovers of God—having a form of godliness but denying its power. Have nothing to do with them.

2 Timothy 3:2-5

Decadence means going morally and spiritually downhill. The modern West is very decadent, as we all know, and its decadence threatens the church, as worldly ways always do. Though we negate secular humanist doctrine, we live by its value system and suffer its symptoms: Man-centeredness as a way of life, with God there to care for me; preoccupation with wealth, luxury, success, and lots of happy sex as means to my fulfillment; unconcern about self-denial, self-control, truthfulness, and modesty; high tolerance of moral lapses, with readiness to make excuses for ourselves and others in the name of charity; indifference to demands for personal and church discipline; prizing ability above character, and ducking out of personal responsibilities—is any of that Christian? The truth is that we have met the secular humanist enemy, and ethically, it is us. Shame on us? Yes, every time.

"Decadence a la Mode," 13

REFLECT: The church is threatened by human-centeredness and self-seeking.

Meanwhile, the people in Judah said, "The strength of the laborers is giving out, and there is so much rubble that we cannot rebuild the wall."

Nehemiah 4:10

Pastors and spiritual leaders today whose concerns extend beyond maintenance to mission, and who seek a genuine extending of God's kingdom, find themselves faced again and again with what has to be classed as attitudinal rubble—laziness, unbelief, procrastination, cynicism, self-absorption, infighting, and fence-sitting among the Lord's people, and many similar factors that hinder and obstruct spiritual advance. These make the task of leadership twice as hard as it would otherwise be, and the going twice as slow. Nehemiah must have felt the temptation to give up hope as strongly as did any of those he led, just as Moses must have felt it at the people's folly in the wilderness wanderings, Paul at the inroads of heresy, immaturity, and immorality in the churches he planted, and Jesus at the spiritual dullness of his own closest disciples. Yet they all kept going, just as true spiritual leaders today will keep going despite misunderstanding, malice, and hostility in all its forms.

A Passion for Faithfulness, 108-109

REFLECT: Leadership is difficult because God's people are imperfect.

I beat my body and make it my slave so that after I have preached to others, I myself will not be disqualified for the prize.
1 Corinthians 9:27

It is a mistake to think that growth in grace is automatic if you are a religious professional. In reality, being a Christian professional makes it harder to grow spiritually rather than easier. Since professionals are expected, as we may say, to perform—to fulfill roles—the temptation to settle for an appropriate form of mask-wearing role play, in which one's own personhood is kept out of sight, is very strong. Professional identity then eats up personal identity, so that one is no longer closely related to anyone, neither to people nor to God. So one is lonely. Even worse, since life is relationships, and behind one's mask one has distanced oneself from relationships, one is shrinking rather than growing as a person. And one cannot grow in grace while one is shrinking overall. All Christians need God's help to know who they are and to live with him and with their own human intimates in honesty, integrity, and vulnerability. But Christian professionals need this help most of all.

Rediscovering Holiness, 185

REFLECT: Growth in grace is more difficult for the Christian professional—the ordained or lay minister—than for others.

*One of you says, "I follow Paul"; another, "I follow Apollos";
another, "I follow Cephas"; still another, "I follow Christ." Is
Christ divided?*

1 Corinthians 1:12-13

Division in the church is pathological, a form of spiritual ill
health in Christ's body. Why does this illness of division exist?
The question is not hard to answer: it exists because of Satan
and sin. Satan keeps pace with God in attempting to spoil
what God is doing. God is busy uniting all sorts and conditions of people out of every nation and tongue, and Satan is
trying to stop this from happening. He wants to divide the
family, split the body, spoil the fellowship. And sin? Sin in our
imperfectly sanctified nature is what you might call an
instinct for division. The first thing that sin did when it came
into the world was to estrange Adam and Eve from each
other. Then it caused Cain to kill Abel. Alas, the sinful
impulse, whenever let loose, is still divisive. So the people of
God fail to practice unity as they should, and Christ appears
to be divided.

"Divisions in the Church," 38

REFLECT: Satan divides, but God brings together.

Because of your wrath there is no health in my body;
my bones have no soundness because of my sin.
My guilt has overwhelmed me
like a burden too heavy to bear.

Psalm 38:3-4

Our spiritual life is at best a fragile convalescence, easily disrupted. Modern Christians egg each other on to testify that where once we were blind, deaf, and indeed dead so far as God was concerned, now through Christ we have been brought to life, radically transformed, and blessed with spiritual health. Thank God, there is real truth in that. But spiritual health means being holy and whole. To the extent that we fall short of being holy and whole, we are not fully healthy either. When there are tensions, strains, perversities, and disappointments in the Christian fellowship, it helps to remember that no Christian, and no church, ever has the clean bill of spiritual health that would match the total physical well-being for which today's fitness seekers labor. To long for total spiritual well-being is right and natural, but to believe that one is anywhere near it is to be utterly self-deceived.

"The Reality Cure," 34-35

REFLECT: No individual or Christian fellowship is totally healthy.

We do not dare to classify or compare ourselves with some who commend themselves. When they measure themselves by themselves and compare themselves with themselves, they are not wise.
2 Corinthians 10:12

Christ finds us in different places in term of our character and personal story, and he works on us by his Spirit in the place where he finds us. Though one of us may be naturally nice in a way that another is not, we are all at the deepest level wrecked vessels spiritually, each needing a divine salvage operation geared to the specifics of our condition. No wonder, then, if God's health-giving, growth-producing work of sanctification is differently shaped in detail, and appears to proceed at different speeds, in different lives.

Since so much of this work, in others and in ourselves, goes on in the heart, below the level of consciousness, we can never measure how far it has gotten, or how far it still has to go, in any single case. Any comparisons we make between its progress in one and in another are bound to be ignorant and fallacious, so we had better learn not to make them.

Rediscovering Holiness, 184

REFLECT: Comparisons are misleading; my focus should be on God's work in *my* life.

You, then, why do you judge your brother? Or why do you look down on your brother? For we will all stand before God's judgment seat.

Romans 14:10

The way to view other Christians—preachers, pastors, academics, colleagues, parents, spouses, children, or whomever—is to focus on what by God's grace they are and have, rather than to dwell constantly on what they are not and do not have. God likes variety; cloning is not his way. In the order both of creation and of redemption, different people receive from him different abilities, and with them, different personal priorities. We should enlarge our minds and stretch our sympathies to a positive valuation of every gift and mode of wisdom that our Lord has put in his church, and we should tell ourselves firmly that narrowing our focus here, even when it is zeal for our ministry that leads us to do so, is not a virtue but a weakness tending to become a vice.

"The Whale and the Elephant," 11

REFLECT: If I focus on people's gifts instead of their deficiencies, I will begin to see how Christ is building his church.

My son, keep your father's commands
and do not forsake your mother's teaching....
For these commands are a lamp,
this teaching is a light,
and the corrections of discipline
are the way to life.

Proverbs 6:20, 23

The word "discipline," in a church context, conveys to many minds nothing more than the idea of harsh judicial processes; but I use it in its historic Christian sense, which is much broader and has a different focus. It comes from a Latin verb that means "to learn," and it signifies the process of educating and training whereby children become wise and mature adults. Learning through the educator's direction is the basic idea, and the correcting of error only comes into it as a means of directing to what is true and good. Coaches in sports harp on what one does wrong in order to get one into the habit of doing things right, and a primary reason why punitive discipline—admonition, barring from the Lord's Table, and disfellowshipping—has to be practiced in the church is to lead erring souls to repent and forsake what was wrong in their lives. So discipline should be seen as essentially educational and pastoral rather than judicial and punitive. It is a matter of putting people on the right track rather than of memorializing the fact that they were once on the wrong one.

A Passion for Faithfulness, 179-180

REFLECT: Church discipline is a way of getting people back on track.

To each one of us grace has been given as Christ apportioned it.... He...gave some to be apostles, some to be prophets, some to be evangelists, and some to be pastors and teachers, to prepare God's people for works of service, so that the body of Christ may be built up.

Ephesians 4:7, 11-12

Three certainties about spiritual gifts stand out. First, a spiritual gift is an ability in some way to express, celebrate, display, and so communicate Christ. We are told that gifts, rightly used, build up Christians and churches. But only knowledge of God in Christ builds up, so each gift must be an ability from Christ to show and share Christ in an upbuilding way. Second, gifts are of two types. There are gifts of speech and of loving, practical helpfulness. No thought of superiority of one gift over another may enter in. However much gifts differ as forms of human activity, all are of equal dignity, and the only question is whether one properly uses the gift one has. Third, no Christian is giftless, and it is everyone's responsibility to find, develop, and fully use whatever capacities for service God has given.

Concise Theology, 227-228

REFLECT: All Christians have gifts that can build up the church in Christ.

Each one should use whatever gift he has received to serve others, faithfully administering God's grace in its various forms.

1 Peter 4:10

No Christian is self-sufficient; we all need each other and what God has given each other. We must learn, therefore, to express our love in the give-and-take of Christian fellowship, and this loving fellowship must take the form of ministry—literally, service. In this basic sense, the church's ministry is a vocation to which every Christian is called. It is for this life of ministry, in which every part of the body is called to make its own contribution, that God gives spiritual gifts, the ability to express and communicate in some way one's knowledge of Christ and his grace. Gifts and ministry are correlative: God gives each Christian a gift, not primarily for personal use, but for others, to be used for their good in the fellowship of the body's life. All can serve others in some way, and all are called to do so; and such service, whatever its form, is an exercise of gifts.

"The Holy Spirit and the Local Congregation," 105-106

REFLECT: Spiritual gifts are given for ministry.

Direct my footsteps according to your word;
let no sin rule over me.

Psalm 119:133

How does one find one's own proper ministry task once one has found the Lord? Four factors ordinarily come together in this process. We shall take them one at a time.

First, there is the *biblical* factor. This is in a broad sense directional, setting before us goals and guidelines and a scale of values for shaping our lives. The Bible tells us in general terms what is and is not worth doing, what sorts of action God encourages and what sorts he forbids, and what are the things that need to be done in serving the needs of saints and sinners. Hereby it says to us in effect: it is within these limits, in pursuit of these goals, in observance of these priorities, that you will find your ministry. The biblical factor is basic, in the sense that God never leads us to transgress any scriptural boundaries, and if we think we are being so led we need someone with a Bible in his hand to tell us we are deluded.

A Passion for Faithfulness, 55

REFLECT: My true ministry will be in harmony with biblical directives and priorities.

Those who are led by the Spirit of God are sons of God.
Romans 8:14

How does God guide us into the specific roles for which he has gifted us? After the biblical factor comes the *pneumatic* factor. By this I mean the God-given desires of the spiritually renewed heart, plus any particular nudges that the Holy Spirit may give or any special burdens of concern that he may impose over and above those general desires. Here we reach an area where self-deception is easy and mistakes often get made, but it would be wrong to deprecate openness to the Holy Spirit on that account. Christians vary as to how much or how little of this nudging they experience; but it would be perverse either for those who know more of it to treat as unspiritual those who confessedly know less of it, or for those who know less of it to treat as self-deceived those who claim to know more of it. We may not ourselves often be guided by this kind of inner nudge, but to discourage Christians from being open to it, as has sometimes been done, is radically Spirit-quenching.

A Passion for Faithfulness, 55-56

REFLECT: The Spirit may nudge me toward a particular ministry.

They must first be tested; and then if there is nothing against them, let them serve as deacons.

1 Timothy 3:10

The third factor for finding one's own ministry task, after the biblical and pneumatic factors, is the *body* factor: that is, the discipline of submitting such leading towards ministry as we believe ourselves to have received to the body of Christ in its local manifestation. The reason for this is that our self-judgment as to whether we are fit and able for ministry roles that attract us is not to be trusted; again and again our own self-assessments prove inaccurate. Self-judgments have to be judged and checked by others. When God calls, he equips; when the equipment is lacking, God's call is not to what the candidate had in mind, but to something else. It can work the other way, too: persons fitted for a ministry may not realize it and may need to allow others within the body—pastors, peers, or whomever—to suggest to them what that ministry should be. For it is within the body that each person's true calling will be discerned.

A Passion for Faithfulness, 56-57

REFLECT: Christ's body, the church, will help me discern the ministry to which God calls me.

I do not want you to be unaware, brothers, that I planned many times to come to you (but have been prevented from doing so until now) in order that I might have a harvest among you, just as I have had among the other Gentiles.

Romans 1:13

How does one find one's own proper ministry task? First, one knows well the limits, goals, and priorities set out in the Bible. Second, one remains open to the Holy Spirit's nudging. Third, one submits one's self-judgments to a cross-section of the Christian fellowship. The fourth and final factor is that of *opportunity*. If the God of providence is calling someone to a particular ministry, he will so overrule that person's situation that he or she will be able to move into that ministry. If circumstances make such a move impossible, the right conclusion is that though God indeed has a ministry for this person, it is not what was originally thought, because of the way the door of circumstances has been closed.

A Passion for Faithfulness, 57

REFLECT: When God calls me, he makes it possible for me to move in the direction he is leading.

Sow your seed in the morning,
and at evening let not your hands be idle,
for you do not know which will succeed,
whether this or that,
or whether both will do equally well.

Ecclesiastes 11:6

The success syndrome is an infection that has spread right through the whole Western world, so that its prevalence among Christian people, though distressing, is hardly surprising. The world's idea that everyone, from childhood up, should be able to succeed at all times in measurable ways, and that it is a great disgrace not to, hangs over the Christian community like a pall of acrid smoke; and if the spiritual counterpart of agonized coughing, lung pain, and shortness of breath should result, no one should be surprised. Those who want to become Christ's agents in building his church now feel they have to have track records that show them as successes in everything to which they ever put their hand. So the impostors have a field day: anything that in the short term looks like triumph is equated with personal success, and anything that in the short term looks like disaster is seen as failure. Successful looking performance at all costs becomes the goal, and unreality creeps into people's view of themselves as a result.

A Passion for Faithfulness, 206

REFLECT: The church is built by obedience, not performance.

Let us not become weary in doing good, for at the proper time we will reap a harvest if we do not give up.

Galatians 6:9

Our calling is not to success but to faithfulness, whatever our role in the body of Christ. Christ will build his church, using us as he wills, in ways that involve the appearance of triumph and disaster over and over again. Our part is not to let either appearance fool us, but to maintain an unflinching fidelity to the particular tasks and roles we know we have been given to fulfill, all for the honoring and pleasing of the Father, the Son, and the Holy Spirit, who by their joint action are carrying forward the entire building process. Such faithfulness—the grace of zealously keeping on whether discouraged or encouraged, with a humility that stays constant when encouraged no less than when discouraged—is a lesson that we shall only ever learn through divine help, help that is found by keeping close to Jesus Christ.

A Passion for Faithfulness, 212

REFLECT: God calls the church to faithfulness, with humility.

MAY

God answers prayer within
his sovereign will.

I will extol the LORD at all times;
his praise will always be on my lips.
My soul will boast in the LORD;
let the afflicted hear and rejoice.
Glorify the LORD with me;
let us exalt his name together.

Psalm 34:1-3

God has shown his wisdom, love, and power in creation, providence, and redemption, and all of his self-revelation calls for constant praise, since it is infinitely praiseworthy. Man's vocation, in essence and at heart, is to give his Maker glory (praise) for all the glories (powers and performances) that God shows him. The chief end of man is to glorify God, and in so doing to enjoy him, and that for ever, as the first answer of the Westminster Shorter Catechism puts it. God's doings should be known and celebrated everywhere, and when his rational human creatures fail to honor him in this way, they rob him of his due, as well as robbing themselves of their own highest happiness. For human life was meant to be an infinitely enriching love affair with the Creator, an unending exploration of the delights of doxology, and nothing makes up for the absence of those joys that come from praise.

"Introduction: Why Preach?," 25

REFLECT: "The chief end of man is to glorify God..."

I glory in Christ Jesus in my service to God. I will not venture to speak of anything except what Christ has accomplished through me.

Romans 15:17-18

Christianity teaches us not to pretend that we lack qualities which we know very well that we have, but to acknowledge that all we have is God's gift to us, so that he should be praised and admired for it rather than we. The test is to ask yourself how pleased, or how displeased, you become if God is praised while you are not, and equally if you are praised while God is not. The mature Christian is content not to have glory given to him, but it troubles him if men are not glorifying God. It pained the dying Puritan, Richard Baxter, the outstanding devotional writer of his day, when visitors praised him for his books. "I was but a pen in God's hand," he whispered, "and what praise is due to a pen?" That shows the mentality of the mature; they want to cry every moment, "Give glory to God!—for it is his due, and his alone!"

Growing in Christ, 213

REFLECT: My life is to give glory to God, not to myself.

I have come down from heaven not to do my will but to do the will of him who sent me.

John 6:38

Egocentricity is the central core of the image of Satan in fallen humanity. This can be described as unwillingness to see oneself as existing for the Creator's pleasure and instead establishing oneself as the center of everything. Pride is the classic Christian name for this self-asserting, self-worshiping syndrome, of which "my will be done" is the implicit motto. Though egocentric pride may adopt the form of Christianity, it corrupts Christianity's substance and spirit. It tries to manage God and harness him to our goals. This reduces religion to magic. *Theocentricity* that repudiates egocentricity, recognizing that in the fundamental sense we exist for God rather than he for us and worshiping him accordingly, is basic to real godliness. Without this radical shift from self-centeredness to God-centeredness, any show of religion is phony.

Hot Tub Religion, 71-72

REFLECT: True religion is God-centered, not self-centered.

Say among the nations, "The LORD reigns."
The world is firmly established, it cannot be moved;
he will judge the peoples with equity.

Psalm 96:10

God exercises purposeful management and control over everything everywhere all the time, and nothing happens without his being involved. "The Lord *reigns*." We should believe, even when we cannot as yet see, that all events will eventually appear to us, from one standpoint or another, as matter for praise. God knows what he is doing, and is in the process of achieving something wise and good every moment. The glory of God through praise for his manifested praiseworthiness is God's goal throughout, and is guaranteed to be the final result.

"Westminster and the Roller Coaster Ride," 8

REFLECT: God is involved in everything that happens.

The Most High is sovereign over the kingdoms of men and gives them to anyone he wishes and sets over them the lowliest of men.
Daniel 4:17

The assertion of God's absolute sovereignty in creation, providence, and grace is basic to biblical belief. We are constantly told that the LORD reigns as king, exercising total dominion: he wills as he chooses and carries out all that he wills, and none can thwart his plans. That God's rational creatures, angelic and human, have free agency (power of personal decision as to what they shall do) is also clear in Scripture throughout; we would not be moral beings, answerable to God the judge, were it not so. Yet the fact of free agency confronts us with mystery, inasmuch as God's control over our free, self-determined activities is as complete as it is over anything else, and how this can be we do not know. Regularly, however, God exercises his sovereignty by letting things take their course, rather than by miraculous intrusions of a disruptive sort.

Concise Theology, 33-34

REFLECT: God is sovereign over all, and yet I have free agency.

The LORD is our judge,
the LORD is our lawgiver,
the LORD is our king;
it is he who will save us.

Isaiah 33:22

Scripture teaches that, as King, God orders and controls all things, human actions among them, in accordance with his own eternal purpose. Scripture also teaches that, as Judge, he holds every person responsible for the choices he makes and the courses of action he pursues. God's sovereignty and man's responsibility are taught us side by side in the same Bible; sometimes, indeed, in the same text. Both are thus guaranteed to us by the same divine authority; both, therefore, are true. It follows that they must be held together, and not played off against each other. Man is a responsible moral agent, though he is also divinely controlled; man is divinely controlled, though he is also a responsible moral agent.

Evangelism and the Sovereignty of God, 22-23

REFLECT: God is sovereign, and yet I am responsible.

God has mercy on whom he wants to have mercy, and he hardens whom he wants to harden.

Romans 9:18

Is not God's sovereignty—his power to fulfill his purposes—limited by the free will of man? No. Man's power of spontaneous and responsible choice is a created thing, an aspect of the mystery of created human nature, and God's power to fulfill his purposes is not limited by anything that he has made. Just as he works out his will through the functioning of the physical order, so he works out his will through the functioning of our psychological makeup. In no case is the integrity of the created thing affected, and it is always possible (apart from some miracles) to explain what has happened without reference to the rule of God. But in every case God orders the things that come to pass.

Growing in Christ, 32

REFLECT: God's sovereignty is not limited by human free will.

One of you will say to me: "Then why does God still blame us? For who resists his will?"

Romans 9:19

Without violating the nature of created realities, or reducing man's activity to robot level, God still "works out everything in conformity with the purpose of his will" (Ephesians 1:11). But surely in that case what we think of as our free will is illusory and unreal? That depends on what you mean. It is certainly illusory to think that our wills are free only if they operate apart from God. But free will in the sense of "free agency"—that is, the power of spontaneous, self-determining choice—is real. As a fact of creation, an aspect of our humanness, it exists, as all created things do, in God. How God sustains it and overrules it without overriding it is his secret; but that he does so is certain, both from our own conscious experience of making decisions, and also from Scripture's sobering insistence that we are answerable to God for our actions, because in the moral sense they really are ours.

Growing in Christ, 32-33

REFLECT: God uses my decisions to work out his will.

The LORD reigns, let the earth be glad;
let the distant shores rejoice.

Psalm 97:1

To know that nothing happens in God's world apart from God's will may frighten the godless, but it stabilizes the saints. It assures them that God has everything worked out, and that everything that happens has a meaning whether or not we can see it at the time. Peter reasoned about the cross this way in the first Christian evangelistic sermon, preached on Pentecost morning. "This man [Jesus] was handed over to you *by God's set purpose and foreknowledge;* and you, with the help of wicked men, put him to death" (Acts 2:23, emphasis added). Knowing that God is on the throne upholds one under pressure and in the face of bewilderment, pain, hostility, and events that seem not to make sense.

Hot Tub Religion, 46

REFLECT: Everything that happens has a meaning.

"My thoughts are not your thoughts,
neither are your ways my ways,"
declares the LORD.
"As the heavens are higher than the earth,
so are my ways higher than your ways
and my thoughts than your thoughts."

Isaiah 55:8-9

Ought we to be surprised when we find ourselves baffled by what God is doing? No! We must not forget who we are. We are not gods; we are creatures, and no more than creatures. As creatures, we have no right or reason to expect that at every point we shall be able to comprehend the wisdom of our Creator. The King has made it clear to us that it is not his pleasure to disclose all the details of his policy to his human subjects. God has disclosed his mind and will so far as we need to know it for practical purposes, and we are to take what he has disclosed as a complete and adequate rule for our faith and life. But there will remain things that he has not made known and that, in this life at least, he does not intend us to discover. And the reasons behind God's providential dealings sometimes fall into this category.

Hot Tub Religion, 19-20

REFLECT: Created beings do not always understand the ways of their Creator.

The LORD said to Job:
"Will the one who contends with the Almighty correct him?
Let him who accuses God answer him! ...
Brace yourself like a man;
I will question you,
and you shall answer me.
Would you discredit my justice?
Would you condemn me to justify yourself?"

Job 40:1-2, 7-8

Einstein using baby talk could make himself known to a two-year-old as a kind and friendly adult, yet the child would have no notion how all his ideas, plans, values, priorities, and judgments of possibilities fitted together in his mind, partly because he would not have talked to the child about these things and partly because the child could not have understood him if he had. Now with God we are in the position of the two-year-old. God has talked and talks still to us in the human language of the written Scriptures, and from what he tells us that he said and did we truly know him. Yet we may be sure that most of what God himself knows to be true regarding his own ideas, plans, values, priorities, and judgments of possibilities is unknown to us. The God of the Bible is the great and undomesticated God who, as he made plain to Job, is under no obligation to explain to us all his reasons for doing what he does.

God's Words, 165

REFLECT: I know all I need to know about God's will, but there is much I will never understand.

Then Job replied to the LORD:
"I know that you can do all things;
no plan of yours can be thwarted.
You asked, 'Who is this that obscures my counsel
without knowledge?'
Surely I spoke of things I did not understand,
things too wonderful for me to know."

Job 42:1-3

Scripture tells us all that we need to know for faith and godliness. But at no point dare we imagine that the thoughts about God that Scripture teaches us take the full measure of his reality. The fact that God condescends and accommodates himself to us in his revelation certainly makes possible clarity and sureness of understanding. Equally certain, however, it involves limitation in the revelation itself. If we fail to acknowledge God's incomprehensibility beyond the limits of what he has revealed, we shrink him in thought down to our size. The process is sometimes described as putting God in a box. It is certainly proper to stress that scriptural revelation is rational. But the most thoroughgoing Bible believers are sometimes required, like Job, to go on adoring God when we do not specifically understand what he is doing and why he is doing it.

"What Do You Mean When You Say God?," 31

REFLECT: God is greater than my understanding.

A time is coming and has now come when the true worshipers will worship the Father in spirit and truth, for they are the kind of worshipers the Father seeks.

John 4:23

Worship—in the sense of telling God his worth by speech and song and celebrating his worth in his presence by proclamation and meditation—has been largely replaced, at least in the West, by a form of entertainment calculated to give worshipers the equivalent of a sauna or a Jacuzzi experience and send them away feeling relaxed and tuned up at the same time. As all that glitters is not gold, so all that makes us feel happy and strong is not worship. The question is not whether a particular liturgical form is used, but whether a God-centered as distinct from a man-centered perspective is maintained—whether, in other words, the sense that man exists for God rather than God for man is cherished or lost. Such worship can occur only when the Holy Spirit is taken seriously as the One who through the written word of Scripture shows us the love and glory of the Son and the Father and draws us into personal communion with both.

"Introduction: On Being Serious
about the Holy Spirit," xiii-xiv

REFLECT: True worship focuses on God.

Do not be anxious about anything, but in everything, by prayer and petition, with thanksgiving, present your requests to God.
Philippians 4:6

In prayer you ask for things and give thanks for things. Why? Because you recognize that God is the author and source of all the good that you have had already, and all the good that you hope for in the future. This is the fundamental philosophy of Christian prayer. The prayer of a Christian is not an attempt to force God's hand, but a humble acknowledgment of helplessness and dependence. When we are on our knees, we know that it is not we who control the world; it is not in our power, therefore, to supply our needs by our own independent efforts; every good thing that we desire for ourselves and for others must be sought from God, and will come, if it comes at all, as a gift from his hands. This is all luminously clear to us when we are actually praying. In effect, therefore, what we do every time we pray is to confess our own impotence and God's sovereignty. The very fact that a Christian prays is thus proof positive that he believes in the Lordship of his God.

Evangelism and the Sovereignty of God, 11-12

REFLECT: When I pray, I recognize that all good things are gifts from God.

One day Jesus was praying in a certain place. When he finished, one of his disciples said to him, "Lord, teach us to pray, just as John taught his disciples."

Luke 11:1

Praying, like singing, is something you learn to do, not by reading books, but by actually doing it; and it is so natural and spontaneous an activity that you can become quite proficient in it without ever reading it up. Yet, as voice training helps you to sing better, so others' experience and advice can help you pray to better purpose. The Bible is full of models for prayer: 150 patterns of praise, petition, and devotion are contained in the Psalter, and many more examples of proper praying are recorded too, along with much teaching on the subject. We should certainly not content ourselves with parroting off other people's prayers, nor would God be content if we did. But as another pianist's interpretation of a piece can help a budding musician to see how he can best play it, so we are helped to find our own way in prayer by seeing how others have prayed, and indeed by praying with them. And overarching everything we have the Lord's Prayer as our guide.

Growing in Christ, 157

REFLECT: The Psalms and the Lord's Prayer are models to guide my own prayer.

This... is how you should pray: "Our Father in heaven, hallowed be your name, your kingdom come, your will be done on earth as it is in heaven. Give us today our daily bread. Forgive us our debts, as we also have forgiven our debtors. And lead us not into temptation, but deliver us from the evil one."

Matthew 6:9-13

The Lord's Prayer is offering us model answers to the series of questions God puts to us to shape our conversation with him. Thus: "Who do you take me for, and what am I to you?" *(Our Father in heaven.)* "That being so, what is it that you really want most?" *(The hallowing of your name; the coming of your kingdom; to see your will known and done.)* "So what are you asking for right now, as a means to that end?" *(Provision, pardon, protection.)* "How can you be so bold and confident in asking for these things?" *(Because we know you can do it and when you do it, it will bring you glory!)* Sometimes when we pray we feel there is nobody there to listen. What finally dispels this temptation is a fresh realization (Spirit-given, for sure) that God is actually questioning us in the way described, requiring us to tell him honestly how we think of him and what we want from him and why.

Growing in Christ, 160-161

REFLECT: The Lord's Prayer is prayed best by someone who wants to be Christ's fully obedient subject, used by him to extend the kingdom.

Do not call anyone on earth "father," for you have one Father, and he is in heaven.

Matthew 23:9

Knowing that our Father God is in heaven, or (putting it the other way round) knowing that God in heaven is our Father, is meant to increase our wonder, joy, and sense of privilege at being his children and being given the "hot line" or prayer for communication with him. "Hot line" it truly is, for though he is Lord of the worlds, he always has time for us; his eye is on everything every moment, yet we always have his full attention whenever we call on him. Let your thoughts move to and fro like an accelerating pendulum, taking ever wider swings. "He's my Father—and he's God in heaven; he's God in heaven—and he's my Father! It's beyond belief—but it's true!" Grasp this, or rather, let it grasp you; then tell God what you feel about it; and that will be the worship which our Lord wanted to evoke when he gave us this thought pattern for the invocation of the One who is both his Father and ours.

Growing in Christ, 168-169

REFLECT: God, ruler of the universe and maker of heaven and earth, is my Father.

Your will be done on earth as it is in heaven.

Matthew 6:10

I cannot sincerely ask for the doing of God's will without denying myself, for when we get down to the business of everyday living, we regularly find that it is our will rather than his we want to do or to see happening. Nor can I pray this prayer without dedicating myself to keep loyal to God in face of all the opposition which in the fallen world I regularly meet. Luther expounded the words like this: "Let thy will be done, O Father, not the will of the devil, or of any of those who would overthrow thy holy Word or hinder the coming of thy kingdom; and grant that all we may have to endure for its sake may be borne with patience and overcome, so that our poor flesh may not yield or give way from weakness or laziness."

Growing in Christ, 179-180, 216

REFLECT: Do I happily take God's will of command for my rule, and God's will of events for my destiny, knowing (by faith) that both are supremely good?

He went away a second time and prayed, "My Father, if it is not possible for this cup to be taken away unless I drink it, may your will be done."

Matthew 26:42

Here more clearly than anywhere the purpose of prayer becomes plain: not to make God do my will (which is practicing magic), but to bring my will into line with his (which is what it means to practice true religion). See what this petition meant when Jesus voiced it in Gethsemane. The incarnate Lord was in the grip of mind-blowing horror, evoked not just by the expectation of physical pain and outward disgrace (strong men can bear these things in a good cause without too much ado), but by the prospect of being *made sin* and forsaken by his Father on the cross. "Never man feared death like this man," said Luther, truly; and this was why. His whole being shrank from it; yet his prayer remained "not as I will, but as you will" (Matthew 26:39).What it cost him to pray thus we shall never know. What it may cost us to accept God's will we cannot say either—which is, perhaps, as well.

Growing in Christ, 179-180, 216

REFLECT: Is there any matter in which I am flying in the face of God's will of command, excusing myself on the grounds of there being other commands which I faithfully keep? If so, what will I now do about it?

Give us each day our daily bread.

Luke 11:3

J. B. Phillips correctly rendered this clause "give us this (each) day the bread we need." We are told to ask for bread, as the Israelites were told to gather manna, on a day-to-day basis: the Christian way is to live in constant dependence on God, a day at a time. Also, we are to ask for the bread we *need;* that is, for the supply of necessities, not luxuries we can do without. This petition does not sanctify greed! Moreover, we must as we pray be prepared to have God show us, by his providential response of not giving what we sought, that we did not really need it after all.

Growing in Christ, 189

REFLECT: When I have prayed for today's bread, will I then believe that what comes to me, much or little, is God's answer? Will I be content with it, and grateful for it?

Lead us not into temptation.

Luke 11:4

God does and must tempt (in the sense of "test") us regularly, to prove what is in us and show how far we have got. His purpose in this is wholly constructive, to strengthen us and help us forward. Why, then, if temptation is beneficial, should we ask to be spared it? For three reasons. First, whenever God tests us for our good, Satan tries to exploit the situation for our ruin. Second, the pressures in times of trial can be so appalling that no sane Christian can do other than shrink from them, just as one shrinks from the thought of having cancer. Third, knowledge of our own proven weakness, thickheadedness, and all-round vulnerability in spiritual matters compels us to cry, in humility and self-distrust, "Lord, if it be possible, *please*, no temptation!" Temptation may be our lot, but only a fool will make it his preference. When it comes, as it inevitably will, do not doubt God's power to deliver from the evil it brings, and to "keep you from falling" (Jude 24) as you pick your way through it.

Growing in Christ, 196, 198

REFLECT: When you are not conscious of temptation, pray "lead us not into temptation"; and when you are conscious of it, pray "deliver us from evil."

O LORD, you have searched me
and you know me.
You know when I sit and when I rise;
you perceive my thoughts from afar.

Psalm 139:1-2

It is by our prayers that we are known—to God, if not to humans. "What a man is alone on his knees before God," said Murray McCheyne, "that he is, and no more." In this case, however, we should add, "and no less." For secret prayer is the veritable mainspring of the godly person's life. When we speak of prayer, we are not referring to the prim, proper, stereotyped, self-regarding formalities that sometimes pass for the real thing. The godly person does not play at prayer. His heart is in it. Prayer to him is his chief work. His prayer is consistently the expression of his strongest and most constant desire. By this God knows his saints, and by this we may know ourselves.

Hot Tub Religion, 37-38

REFLECT: Prayer is the chief work of the godly person.

Put on the full armor of God so that you can take your stand against the devil's schemes. And pray in the Spirit on all occasions with all kinds of prayers and requests. With this in mind, be alert and always keep on praying for all the saints.

Ephesians 6:11, 18

Prayer, though from one standpoint the most natural thing a Christian ever does, since crying to his heavenly Father is a Spirit-wrought instinct in him, is always a battle against distractions, discouragements, and deadenings from Satan and from our own sinfulness. God may actually resist us when we pray in order that we in turn may resist and overcome his resistance, and so be led into deeper dependence on him and greater enrichment from him at the end of the day (think of wrestling Jacob, and clamoring Job, and the parable of the unjust judge). I see true prayer, like all true obedience, as a constant struggle in which you make headway by effort against what opposes, and however much you progress you are always aware of imperfection, incompleteness, and how much further you have to go.

"My Path of Prayer," 58-59

REFLECT: Prayer requires hard work.

If you believe, you will receive whatever you ask for in prayer.
Matthew 21:22

God's promises to answer the prayers of his own children are categorical and inclusive. It must then be wrong to think that a flat no is ever the whole of his response to reverent petitions from Christians who seek his glory and others' welfare. The truth must be this: God always acts positively when a believer lays a situation of need before him, but he does not always act in the way or at the speed asked for. In meeting the need he does what he knows to be best when he knows it is best to do it. Christ's word to Paul, "My grace is sufficient for you, for power is made perfect in weakness" (2 Corinthians 12:9), meant no, but not simply no: though it was not what Paul expected, it was a promise of something better than the healing he had sought.

"My Path of Prayer," 63

REFLECT: When I pray, God always meets my need in the way he knows to be best.

Going a little farther, he fell with his face to the ground and prayed, "My Father, if it is possible, may this cup be taken from me. Yet not as I will, but as you will."

Matthew 26:39

Jesus teaches that we may properly press God hard with fervent persistence when we bring needs to him, and that he will answer such prayer in positive terms. But we must remember that God, who knows what is best in a way that we do not, may deny our specific requests as to how the needs should be met. If he does, however, it is because he has something better to give than what we asked for, as was the case when Christ denied Paul healing for the thorn in his flesh (2 Corinthians 12:7-9). To say "Your will be done," surrendering one's own expressed preference to the Father's wisdom as Jesus did in Gethsemane, is the most explicit way of expressing faith in the goodness of what God has planned.

Concise Theology, 188-189

REFLECT: "Your will be done" expresses faith in God's good plan.

In my distress I called to the LORD; I cried to my God for help. From his temple he heard my voice; my cry came before him, into his ears.

Psalm 18:6

Scripture tells us that God gives strength for three things: endurance of strain and pressure, fidelity in serving God and others, and resistance to satanic wiles. The Lord Jesus, who showed this threefold strength to perfection in the days of his flesh, now from his throne imparts it to those who are alive in him. In them the moral and spiritual instincts of Jesus' holy character now seek active expression, and the Holy Spirit acts in their actions to work in them the good works in which the expression of these instincts is seen. But this becomes reality only when Christians feel too weak, mentally, morally, spiritually, and maybe physically too, to rise to the demands of each situation. Then they extend the hand of faith to God as drowning men stretch for the life belt. "Help!" is prayer at its truest, as it is weakness at its most explicit. And it is a prayer that God answers!

"The Way of the Weak Is the Only Healthy Way," 28

REFLECT: God provides strength at my moment of need.

He who doubts is like a wave of the sea, blown and tossed by the wind. That man should not think he will receive anything from the Lord; he is a double-minded man, unstable in all he does.

James 1:6-8

When James says "double-minded" (literally, "two-souled") he means more than "irresolute," "undecided," and "unable to make up his mind," as various modern versions render the word. He is detecting not temperamental ditheriness, but unbelief: doubting—that is, mistrusting—the good will of the God whom one trusts for salvation, prays to, and calls Father. The two-minded person, while professing faith in Christ as divine Savior and Lord, panics under pressure, thinks with his feelings rather than his brains, and concludes that since God evidently no longer cares for him, his prayers for wisdom cannot expect an answer. Yet God is unchanging in his love and free from any shadow of inconstancy. Don't insult him by indulging such unbelief, says James. What, then, is James's answer to double-mindedness? Why, single-mindedness, of course: believing all that God says, not just some of it; putting faith in his faithfulness about everything, joyfully trusting his goodness at all times, and seeking to honor him by consistent holiness. That is true purity of heart, and that is the only life of faith worthy of the name.

"Bringing the Double Mind to Singleness of Faith," 59

REFLECT: The single-minded Christian trusts God, not himself or herself.

I call on you, O God, for you will answer me;
give ear to me and hear my prayer.

Psalm 17:6

Does God really tell us things when we pray? Yes. We shall probably not hear voices, nor feel sudden strong impressions of a message coming through (and we shall be wise to suspect such experiences should they come our way); but as we analyze and verbalize our problems before God's throne, and tell him what we want and why we want it, and think our way through passages and principles of God's written Word bearing on the matter in hand, we shall find many certainties crystallizing in our hearts as to God's view of us and our prayers, and his will for us and others. If you ask, "Why is this or that happening?" no light may come, for "the secret things belong to the LORD our God" (Deuteronomy 29:29); but if you ask, "How am I to serve and glorify God here and now, where I am?" there will always be an answer.

Growing in Christ, 156

REFLECT: In prayer I come to know how God wants me to serve him.

If you,... though you are evil, know how to give good gifts to your children, how much more will your Father in heaven give good gifts to those who ask him!

Matthew 7:11

Can we by petitionary prayer control and direct God's power? The short answer is no, we cannot manipulate God into doing our will when our will is not his. Yet he regularly wills to give blessings in answer to the prayers which, through incentives from Scripture and the burdening of our hearts by his Spirit, he prompts us to make. By this means he achieves two goals together: giving of good gifts to his children, which he loves to do; and enriching of their relationship with him through the special joy and excitement of seeing that the good things were given in response to their petitions. Moreover, there are times—not many, but they do occur— when God gives great assurance as to what to pray for, and great confidence before the event that the prayer will be answered. The memory of such occasions remains as a strong incentive to pray confidently and expectantly about the next need that appears.

Rediscovering Holiness, 230-231

REFLECT: Though I cannot manipulate God, he loves to respond to my prayers by blessing me.

Three times I pleaded with the Lord to take it away from me. But he said to me, "My grace is sufficient for you, for my power is made perfect in weakness."

2 Corinthians 12:8-9

Is it ever right to ask God to show his power by a miracle? Provided that the bottom line of our prayer is "thy will be done," there is nothing improper in our telling God when we think that a miracle—a spectacular coincidence, or a display of the power of the new creation in, for instance, organic healing—would advance his glory and the hallowing of his name. Paul prayed for miraculous healing of his thorn in the flesh. He was not wrong to do so, although as it turned out a miracle was not God's answer to his prayer. We only go wrong if, when we ask for a miracle, we are not prepared to find that God has other ideas. But his power remains undiminished; and although we must recognize that miracles are always unlikely, we need to remember that they are never impossible.

Rediscovering Holiness, 232

REFLECT: Ask for a miracle, but leave the results to God.

"Father, if you are willing, take this cup from me; yet not my will, but yours be done."

Luke 22:42

The truth is not that prayer changes God's mind or twists his arm but rather that our prayer, generated and sustained as it is by God himself, becomes the means of our entering into God's mind. We end up asking him to do what he had planned all along to do, once he had brought us to the point of asking him to do it with an appropriately felt seriousness of concern. If we want to see the power of God at work answering our prayers (and there is something wrong with us if we do not), our task is not to screw ourselves up to a self-induced certainty that what we have chosen to ask for is going to happen, just because we have assured ourselves that it will. Our task is, rather, to seek God's mind about the needs that press on us and to allow him to show us how we should pray "thy will be done"—thus following Jesus' path of prayer in Gethsemane.

Rediscovering Holiness, 232

REFLECT: Prayer brings me into God's will.

JUNE

God wills us to love
and serve others.

Do not store up for yourselves treasures on earth, where moth and rust destroy, and where thieves break in and steal. But store up for yourselves treasures in heaven.... For where your treasure is, there your heart will be also.

Matthew 6:19-21

Christians are sent into the world by their Lord to witness to it about God's Christ and his kingdom and to serve its needs. But they are to do so without falling victim to its materialism, its unconcern about God and the next life, and its prideful pursuit of pleasure, profit, and position to the exclusion of everything else. The world is at present Satan's kingdom, and the outlook and mindset of human societies reflect more of the pride seen in Satan than the humility seen in Christ. Christians, like Christ, are to empathize with people's anxieties and needs in order to serve them and communicate with them effectively. They are to do so, however, on a basis of motivational detachment from this world, through which they are momentarily passing as they travel home to God and in which their single-minded purpose must be to please God.

Concise Theology, 234-235

REFLECT: God calls me to serve others without becoming attached to the world.

Do everything without complaining or arguing, so that you may become blameless and pure, children of God without fault in a crooked and depraved generation, in which you shine like stars in the universe as you hold out the word of life.

Philippians 2:14-16

The commission to publish the gospel and make disciples was never confined to the apostles. Nor is it now confined to the church's ministers. It is a commission that rests upon the whole church collectively, and therefore upon each Christian individually. All God's people are sent to do as the Philippians did, and "hold out the word of life." Every Christian has a God-given obligation to make known the gospel of Christ. And every Christian who declares the gospel message to any fellowman does so as Christ's ambassador and representative, according to the terms of his God-given commission. Such is the authority, and such the responsibility, of the church and of the Christian in evangelism.

Evangelism and the Sovereignty of God, 45-46

REFLECT: I am called to help make Christ's gospel known.

Then [the king] said to his servants, "The wedding banquet is ready.... Go to the street corners and invite to the banquet anyone you find." So the servants went out into the streets and gathered all the people they could find, both good and bad, and the wedding hall was filled with guests.

Matthew 22:8-10

When God sends us to evangelize, he sends us to act as vital links in the chain of his purpose for the salvation of his elect. The fact that he has such a purpose, and that it is a sovereign purpose that cannot be thwarted, does not imply that, after all, our evangelizing is not needed for its fulfillment. In our Lord's parable, the way in which the wedding was furnished with guests was through the action of the king's servants, who went out as they were bidden into the highways and invited in all whom they found there. Hearing the invitation, the passersby came. It is in the same way, and through similar action by the servants of God, that the elect come into the salvation that the Redeemer has won for them.

Evangelism and the Sovereignty of God, 98

REFLECT: God calls me to invite others to his salvation.

Jesus replied: "'Love the Lord your God with all your heart and with all your soul and with all your mind.' This is the first and greatest commandment. And the second is like it: 'Love your neighbor as yourself.'"

Matthew 22:37-39

If our hearts have felt any measure of gratitude for the grace that has saved us from death and hell, then the attitude of compassion and care for our spiritually needy fellowmen ought to come naturally and spontaneously to us. It is a tragic and ugly thing when Christians are reluctant to share the precious knowledge that they have with others whose need of it is just as great as their own. We should not look for excuses for wriggling out of our obligation when occasion offers to talk to others about the Lord Jesus Christ. If we find ourselves trying to evade this responsibility, we need to face ourselves with the fact that in this we are yielding to sin. We need to ask for grace to be truly ashamed of ourselves, and to pray that we may so overflow in love to God that we shall overflow in love to our fellowmen, and so find it an easy and natural and joyful thing to share with them the good news of Christ.

Evangelism and the Sovereignty of God, 77-78

REFLECT: When I am in love with God, I shall find it easy to share the gospel with others.

I planted the seed, Apollos watered it, but God made it grow. So neither he who plants nor he who waters is anything, but only God, who makes things grow.

1 Corinthians 3:6-7

While we must always remember that it is our responsibility to proclaim salvation, we must never forget that it is God who saves. It is God who brings men and women under the sound of the gospel, and it is God who brings them to faith in Christ. Our evangelistic work is the instrument that he uses for this purpose, but the power that saves is not in the instrument: it is in the hand of the One who uses the instrument. We must not at any stage forget that. For if we forget that it is God's prerogative to give results when the gospel is preached, we shall start to think that it is our responsibility to secure them. And if we forget that only God can give faith, we shall start to think that the making of converts depends, in the last analysis, not on God, but on us, and that the decisive factor is the way in which we evangelize. And this line of thought, consistently followed through, will lead us far astray.

Evangelism and the Sovereignty of God, 27

REFLECT: Making converts is God's prerogative, not mine.

I am not ashamed of the gospel, because it is the power of God for the salvation of everyone who believes.

Romans 1:16

No heart is too hard for the grace of God. You yourself, since you became a Christian, have been learning constantly how corrupt and deceitful and perverse your own heart is. Before you became a Christian, your heart was worse; yet Christ has saved you, and that should be enough to convince you that he can save anyone. So persevere in presenting Christ to unconverted people as you find opportunity. You are not on a fool's errand. You are not wasting either your time or theirs. You have no reason to be ashamed of your message, or half-hearted and apologetic in delivering it. You have every reason to be bold, and free, and natural, and hopeful of success. For God can give his truth an effectiveness that you and I cannot give it. God can make his truth triumphant to the conversion of the most seemingly hardened unbeliever. You and I will never write off anyone as hopeless and beyond the reach of God if we believe in the sovereignty of his grace.

Evangelism and the Sovereignty of God, 118

REFLECT: Nobody is beyond God's reach.

Preach the Word; be prepared in season and out of season; correct, rebuke and encourage—with great patience and careful instruction.

2 Timothy 4:2

Whence comes the patience that is so indispensable for evangelistic work? From dwelling on the fact that God is sovereign in grace and that his word does not return to him void; that it is he who gives us such opportunities as we find for sharing our knowledge of Christ with others, and that he is able in his own good time to enlighten them and bring them to faith. God often exercises our patience in this, as in other matters. As he kept Abraham waiting twenty-five years for the birth of his son, so he often keeps Christians waiting for things that they long to see, such as the conversion of their friends. We need patience, then, if we are to do our part in helping others toward faith. And the way for us to develop that patience is to learn to live in terms of our knowledge of the free and gracious sovereignty of God.

Evangelism and the Sovereignty of God, 121

REFLECT: I may need to wait patiently for God to show his saving power.

Brothers, pray for us that the message of the Lord may spread rapidly and be honored, just as it was with you.

2 Thessalonians 3:1

We should pray for those whom we seek to win, that the Holy Spirit will open their hearts; and we should pray for ourselves in our own witness, and for all who preach the gospel, that the power and authority of the Holy Spirit may rest upon them. Paul was a great evangelist who had seen much fruit, but Paul knew that every particle of it had come from God, and that unless God continued to work both in him and in those to whom he preached he would never convert another soul. So he pleads for prayer, that his evangelism might still prove fruitful. Pray, he pleads, that the word of the gospel may be glorified through my preaching of it and through its effect in human lives. Pray that it may be used constantly to the conversion of sinners. This, to Paul, is an urgent request, just because Paul sees so clearly that his preaching can save nobody unless God in sovereign mercy is pleased to bless it and use it to this end.

Evangelism and the Sovereignty of God, 123

REFLECT: I should pray for those I seek to win to Christ.

We loved you so much that we were delighted to share with you not only the gospel of God but our lives as well, because you had become so dear to us.

1 Thessalonians 2:8

Evangelism is not the only task that our Lord has given us, nor is it a task that we are all called to discharge in the same way. We are not all called to be preachers; we are not all given equal opportunities or comparable abilities for personal dealing with men and women who need Christ. But we all have some evangelistic responsibility which we cannot shirk without failing in love both to our God and to our neighbor. To start with, we all can and should be praying for the salvation of unconverted people, particularly in our family and among our friends and everyday associates. And then we must learn to see what possibilities of evangelism our everyday situation holds, and to be enterprising in our use of them. If we love our neighbor, we shall muster all our initiative and enterprise to find ways and means of doing him good. And one chief way of doing him good is to share with him our knowledge of Christ.

Evangelism and the Sovereignty of God, 78-79

REFLECT: Evangelism is more than preaching.

Whoever wants to become great among you must be your servant, and whoever wants to be first must be your slave—just as the Son of Man did not come to be served, but to serve, and to give his life as a ransom for many.

Matthew 20:26-28

It is artificial and unscriptural to draw a hard and fast dividing line between God's work of transforming a person's character and his work of thrusting that person into ministry—into active service of others, accepted as a task that God has given. Ministry means any form of service, and there are many such forms. Thus,

- being a faithful spouse and a conscientious parent is the form of ministry at home;
- discharging an office, fulfilling a role, and carrying a defined responsibility is the form of ministry (both ordained and lay) in the organized church;
- sustaining pastoral friendships that involve advising, interceding, and supporting is a further form of ministry in Christ; and
- loving care for people at any level of need—physical or mental, material or spiritual—is the true form of ministry in the world.

Rediscovering Holiness, 210-211

REFLECT: All Christians are ministers.

We have different gifts, according to the grace given us. If a man's gift is... serving, let him serve; if it is teaching, let him teach; if it is encouraging, let him encourage; if it is contributing to the needs of others, let him give generously; if it is leadership, let him govern diligently; if it is showing mercy, let him do it cheerfully.

Romans 12:6-8

The New Testament teaches that every Christian has a twofold calling: God calls each of us individually to believe and to serve.

The first calling, so named because the gospel invitation to turn from sin and trust Christ for eternal life is at its heart, is actually a work of power whereby God brings us to faith through the Holy Spirit's action in illuminating us through the gospel and moving us to response.

The second calling is a summons to a task. Paul is emphatic that all Christians are gifted for, and thereby called to, some form of service. All believers are in the Christian ministry, in the sense of being called to find and fulfill the serving role for which God has equipped them. Gifts are given to be used, and a capacity to minister in a particular way constitutes a *prima facie* call to that particular ministry.

A Passion for Faithfulness, 54-55

REFLECT: God calls—and equips—me to believe and to serve.

If you do away with the yoke of oppression, ...
and if you spend yourselves in behalf of the hungry
and satisfy the needs of the oppressed,
then your light will rise in the darkness,
and your night will become like the noonday.
The LORD will guide you always.

Isaiah 58:9-11

It was, I think, Oswald Chambers who said that the need is not the call, but is the occasion for the call, and that is a wise word. There are far more needs in the church and the world than any of us has time or energy to meet, and no one is required to try to relieve them all. Nonetheless, God's call to service will be a call to meet some human need or other, and the sense of what we might and should do to serve God will only crystallize in our hearts out of knowledge of what the needs are. So we should explore the needs that surround us and collect information about them and hold them in our hearts if we want to be led to the particular ministry that God has in mind for us. Cheerful, self-absorbed Christians who fail to do this are not likely to be so led.

A Passion for Faithfulness, 59-60

REFLECT: God's call is always to meet some need.

Even if I am being poured out like a drink offering on the sacrifice and service coming from your faith, I am glad and rejoice with all of you. So you too should be glad and rejoice with me.

Philippians 2:17-18

William Booth, founder and General of the Salvation Army, once gave the Army as a motto for the year the one word, "Others." No one could ever devise a more Christian, indeed Christlike, motto than that. But serving the Lord by being there to seek the good of others, and to help them where they need help, will involve us in being ground up small in the mill of God's providence for others' sake. Augustine expressed this by saying that God's servants have to be "broken and distributed" to feed the hungry; a thought that Oswald Chambers somewhere elaborated by declaring that God turns his agents into broken bread and poured-out wine. Thus it goes, and we must be ready to endure it. True holiness, which is Christ-centered and others-oriented, accepts this without demur.

Rediscovering Holiness, 265

REFLECT: God's servants give themselves to serve others.

My prayer is not that you take them out of the world but that you protect them from the evil one. As you sent me into the world, I have sent them into the world.

John 17:15, 18

Holiness has to do with my relationships. Sometimes it has been thought that a state of isolation and solitude, permanently detached from ordinary human involvements, is a help, or perhaps even a necessity, for the practice of holiness. It is true that holy living calls for regular times of aloneness with God. But the notion that one gains freedom to move ahead with God by cutting oneself off from the communal life of family and church and society does not seem to be true at all. Biblical holiness is unambiguously worldly. Without conforming to the world by becoming materialistic, extravagant, or a grabber and empire builder of any kind, the Christian must operate as a servant of God in the world, serving others for the Lord's sake. The way I relate to others is the essence of my holiness in the sight of God, just as it is one index of it in the sight of men and women.

Rediscovering Holiness, 29-30

REFLECT: The Christian serves God in the world.

We love because he first loved us.

1 John 4:19

New Testament Christianity is essentially a response to the revelation of the Creator as a God of love. God is a tripersonal Being who so loves ungodly humans that the Father has given the Son, the Son has given his life, and Father and Son together now give the Spirit to save sinners from unimaginable misery and lead them into unimaginable glory. Believing in and being overwhelmed by this amazing reality of divine love generates and sustains the love to God and neighbor that Christ's two great commandments require. Our love is to express our gratitude for God's gracious love to us, and to be modeled on it.

Concise Theology, 181

REFLECT: I love God and my neighbor in response to God's love for me.

Do not rejoice that the spirits submit to you, but rejoice that your names are written in heaven.

Luke 10:20

It is right to aspire to use one's God-given gifts in powerful and useful ministry. It is right to want to know what gifts for ministry God has given us. It is right to want to harness them and see them used for the blessing of others as widely as possible. But there is always a danger that the person who sees that God has given him or her a good sprinkling of gifts will be betrayed by that old enemy, self-importance—which is another name for pride. God does not value us according to the number of gifts we have or by their spectacular quality. God does not value us primarily in terms of what we can do—even what we can do in his strength. He values us primarily in terms of what he makes us, characterwise, as he conforms us to Christ by his grace.

Rediscovering Holiness, 216

REFLECT: Beware of pride.

*She opens her arms to the poor
and extends her hands to the needy.*

Proverbs 31:20

It is right to want to be a channel of divine power into other people's lives at their points of need. Neighbor-love seeks the good of the loved ones. For strong neighbor-love to be active in our hearts is a sign of spiritual health. But be careful lest you become one of those people who suffer from the neurosis of needing to be needed—the state of not feeling that you are anything or anybody unless you are able to feel that others cannot get on without you! That is not true neighbor-love, nor is it spiritual health. That is *lack* of spiritual health; it is in fact another form of pride. Our sense of personal worth is to flow, not from our Christian activities, nor from having others depending on us, but from our knowledge that God loved us enough to redeem us at the cost of Calvary.

Rediscovering Holiness, 216-217

REFLECT: Beware of the neurosis of having to feel needed.

When they had finished eating, Jesus said to Simon Peter, "Simon son of John, do you truly love me more than these?" "Yes, Lord," he said, "you know that I love you." Jesus said, "Feed my lambs."

John 21:15

I ask you straight out: How about your relationship with Jesus Christ? Do you love him? Are you showing that you love him? Words are cheap, and anyone can say that he or she loves Jesus. Anyone can sing it cheerfully. But Jesus says to us that we have to prove it by loving others for his sake. That is what he told Peter.

Peter had said before that he loved Jesus, but then he denied Jesus disastrously. Jesus was now saying to Peter, "Look, Peter, I still want you for a shepherd. I wanted you for a shepherd right from the very beginning. Now, Peter, go out and be a shepherd, and by loving others for my sake you will prove that you love me."

So, I ask you, how is your love for Jesus? Are you showing your love for him by doing the things that he says?

"Shepherds after God's Own Heart," 13-14

REFLECT: I show love for Christ in caring for others.

Love is patient, love is kind. It does not envy, it does not boast, it is not proud. It is not rude, it is not self-seeking, it is not easily angered, it keeps no record of wrongs. Love does not delight in evil but rejoices with the truth. It always protects, always trusts, always hopes, always perseveres.

1 Corinthians 13:4-7

The hallmark of Christian life is Christian love. The measure and test of love to God is wholehearted and unqualified obedience; the measure and test of love to our neighbors is laying down our lives for them. This sacrificial love involves giving, spending, and impoverishing ourselves up to the limit for their well-being. Love is a principle of action rather than of emotion. It is a purpose of honoring and benefiting the other party. It is a matter of doing things for people out of compassion for their need, whether or not we feel personal affection for them. It is by their active love to one another that Jesus' disciples are to be recognized.

Concise Theology, 181-182

REFLECT: Love for others is often marked by sacrifice rather than emotion.

Jesus said, "Peace be with you! As the Father has sent me, I am sending you."

John 20:21

The words Jesus spoke to his first disciples still apply. The universal church, and therefore every local congregation and every Christian in it, is sent into the world to fulfill a definite, defined task. Jesus, the church's Lord, has issued marching orders. The appointed task is twofold. First and fundamentally, it is the work of worldwide witness, disciple making, and church planting. Jesus Christ is to be proclaimed everywhere as God incarnate, Lord, and Savior; and God's authoritative invitation to find life through turning to Christ in repentance and faith is to be delivered to all mankind. Second, all Christians are called to practice deeds of mercy and compassion, a thoroughgoing neighbor-love that responds unstintingly to all forms of human need as they present themselves. Thereby they give credibility to their proclamation of a Savior who makes sinners into lovers of God and of their fellow human beings. Good deeds should be visible to back up good words.

Concise Theology, 223-224

REFLECT: God calls the church to the dual tasks of evangelism and compassion.

They asked him, "What must we do to do the works God requires?" Jesus answered, "The work of God is this: to believe in the one he has sent."

John 6:28-29

Imagine, now, a devoted and gifted Christian woman, whose ministry has been precious to her, finding that for quite a long period the Lord sidelines her so that her potential is not being used. What is going on? Is this spiritual failure? It is probably not spiritual failure at all, but a lesson in Christ's school of holiness. The Lord is reminding her that her life does not depend on finding that people need her. The prime source of her joy must always be the knowledge of God's love for her—the knowledge that though he did not need her, he has chosen to love her freely and gloriously so that she may have the eternal joy of fellowship with him. Regarding her ministry, what matters is that she should be available to him. Then he will decide when and how to put her to service again, and she should leave that with him.

Rediscovering Holiness, 217-218

REFLECT: When I am available to God, he will put me to work as he sees fit.

For this reason I remind you to fan into flame the gift of God, which is in you through the laying on of my hands. For God did not give us a spirit of timidity, but a spirit of power, of love and of self-discipline.

2 Timothy 1:6-7

In saying that to "Timid Tim," Paul is encouraging him to guard against one of the seven deadly sins, the one called *sloth*. The slothful person, instead of investing himself in his work, only goes through the motions. His heart is not completely in it. The word *sloth* also covers "accidie," the classical Christian name for a state of inner toughness and cynicism. Accidie is an inner sourness that makes a person scornful of other people who—as he thinks—naïvely invest themselves 100 percent in work which has begun to disillusion him. Indeed, Paul says to Timothy, if you do not constantly keep in flame that gift which was given you—the life of Christ, the life of heaven that is in you, through the Spirit—you will suffer from accidie and burnout, and it will be your fault. Do not let that happen, Timothy.

"Accidie Will Happen," 159-160

REFLECT: God's Spirit helps me invest myself in the work God has given me to do.

Teach me to do your will,
for you are my God;
may your good Spirit
lead me on level ground.

Psalm 143:10

A vision without a task makes a visionary—head in the clouds, feet off the ground. A task without a vision makes for drudgery—head down, feet caught in the mud. Only a vision with a task produces a ministry. God forbid that our vision should ever fade. God forbid that we should lose our awareness of what God can do in the day when he blesses even the ministry of weak, imperfect creatures like us. Get your vision clear and hold on to it! Keep rekindling each day the gift of God that is in you by refocusing your vision, keeping your priorities clear, and going out into each day with the expectation that the Lord will lead you and do great things for you today. If that is what you are looking for, that is what you will find he does.

"Accidie Will Happen," 160

REFLECT: A vision plus a task produces a ministry.

My son, be strong in the grace that is in Christ Jesus.

2 Timothy 2:1

As we think of the specifics that gospel ministry requires according to the New Testament, we may find our hearts saying, "I could never do that. Lord, don't ever ask me to do that." The Lord may ask us to do any of the things which the first servants of Christ had to do. But when he asks us to do hard things, he promises to equip us to do them. He is the great enabler.

So, when your temperamental limitations are inhibiting you from faithful ministry in some department or other, ask the Lord to enable you to overcome those weaknesses by the grace of the Spirit. Do not settle for yourself as you are, as if you could never be better. God knows you could, and the Spirit is given to make you so. Get your self-image clear, and prove the Spirit's power to enable you to rise to its fulfillment.

"Shepherds after God's Own Heart," 15-16

REFLECT: When God gives me a task, he equips me to do it.

Whatever your hand finds to do, do it with all your might, for in the grave, where you are going, there is neither working nor planning nor knowledge nor wisdom.

Ecclesiastes 9:10

When the Bible talks about work it has in view much more than what we do for money or gain, what we call our job or our employment. In the Bible, work means any exertion of effort that aims at producing a new state of affairs. Such exertions involve our creativity, which is part of God's image in us, and which needs to be harnessed and expressed in action if our nature is to be properly fulfilled. So, for instance, homemaking, shoveling snow, obeying orders, practicing for a performance, darning socks, and answering letters are all focused, intentional exertions that count as work, though none of them necessarily involve contractual employment. Conversely, warbling under the shower to express your sense of euphoria at the feel of the hot water is not work, no matter how much energy you put into it and how much noise you make. If, however, your warbling was learning a part to sing in a choir, that would be work, because of its purpose.

A Passion for Faithfulness, 73-74

REFLECT: Work in the biblical sense is always goal-oriented; it is action with an end in view.

I press on toward the goal to win the prize for which God has called me heavenward in Christ Jesus.

Philippians 3:14

Definition must always be the first step in any successful strategy for accomplishing anything whatever. The first need is to get clear in one's mind what exactly the task is, what are its size and scope, what are its parameters and limits. Then your goals—long-term, mid-term, and short-term—will be clearly set and you will know just what you are aiming at: what you are doing, where you are going, and what will be involved in getting there. Only when a job has been thus defined can you realistically work out means to your end, and only when you are clear about both the end and the means can you expect anyone else to have confidence in your project. When zealous Christians with strong faith allow themselves to go goofy when it comes to orchestrating a cherished enterprise, failure regularly results—not because God is not responsive to faith, but because it is not his way to applaud and bless goofiness.

A Passion for Faithfulness, 83-84

REFLECT: Faith and planning must go together.

It is God who works in you to will and to act according to his good purpose.

Philippians 2:13

Our living should be made up of sequences having the following shape. We begin by considering what we have to do or need to do. Recognizing that without divine help we can do nothing as we should, we confess to the Lord our inability and ask that help be given. Then, confident that prayer has been heard and help will be given, we go to work. And having done what we could we thank God for the ability to do as much as we did and take the discredit for whatever was still imperfect and inadequate, asking forgiveness for our shortcomings and begging for power to do better next time. In this sequence there is room neither for passivity nor for self-reliance. On the contrary, we first trust God, and then on that basis we work as hard as we can and repeatedly find ourselves enabled to do what we know we could not have done alone. That happens through the enabling power of the Holy Spirit, who is the wellspring and taproot of all holy and Christlike action.

Hot Tub Religion, 192-193

REFLECT: The Holy Spirit empowers me when I trust God and go to work.

You have made known to me the path of life;
you will fill me with joy in your presence,
with eternal pleasures at your right hand.

Psalm 16:11

The paradoxical truth is that to seek pleasure, comfort, and happiness is to guarantee that you will miss them all. On the spiritual as on the natural level, these subjective states become heart realities only as by-products that come from focusing on something else, something perceived as valuable, invigorating, and commanding. The seeds of happiness, it has been truly said, grow most strongly in the soil of service. Often the "something else" that wins our allegiance is some-*one* else, a person rather than an abstract concept. That is especially the case where spiritual happiness is concerned. This happiness comes from basking in the knowledge of the redeeming love of the Father and the Son, and showing active loyal gratitude for it. You love God and find yourself happy. Your active attempts to please God funnel the pleasures of his peace into your heart. That is how it goes.

Hot Tub Religion, 64-65

REFLECT: Happiness is a by-product of loving God.

Although I am less than the least of all God's people, this grace was given me: to preach to the Gentiles the unsearchable riches of Christ, and to make plain to everyone the administration of this mystery, which for ages past was kept hidden in God, who created all things.

Ephesians 3:8-9

Christians sometimes find themselves wondering whether their life is worthwhile, whether they are doing anything that is worth doing. They are sometimes concerned about frittering away precious time and opportunities, wondering whether the serious concerns of adult existence in Christ's service have not slipped through their fingers. Sometimes these feelings are justified; Christians sometimes really are wasting their lives. But Christians who invest time, effort, ingenuity, initiative, and prayer in spreading the gospel and helping build the faith of others do not feel this kind of self-doubt. They have no reason to do so. In a dying world, surrounded by fascinating fellow mortals who because of their sins face a lost eternity, nothing is so well worth doing as sharing the good news about Jesus and the salvation he gives. No form of love to our neighbor is so appropriate and, indeed, urgent as evangelism.

Hot Tub Religion, 163

REFLECT: If I am sharing the gospel with others, I know my life has meaning.

[Jesus] said to them, "When you pray, say: 'Father, hallowed be your name, your kingdom come.'"

Luke 11:2

To pray "your kingdom come" is searching and demanding, for one must be ready to add, "and start with me; make me your fully obedient subject. Show me my place among 'workers for the kingdom of God' (Colossians 4:11), and use me, so far as may be, to extend the kingdom and so be your means of answering my prayer." Made sincerely, this is a prayer that the Savior who calls to self-denial and cross-bearing and consent that one's life be lost, one way or another, in serving the gospel, may have his way with us completely. Do we really seek this? Have we faced it? Let us examine ourselves, and so—only so—let us say the Lord's Prayer.

Growing in Christ, 177, 216

REFLECT: I may be called to labor and suffer for the kingdom, so as to become its agent, the means of bringing it into lives and situations where the gates have been locked against God.

JULY

God wills us to enjoy and
care for his created world.

You made him ruler over the works of your hands;
you put everything under his feet:
all flocks and herds, and the beasts of the field,
the birds of the air, and the fish of the sea,
all that swim the paths of the seas.

Psalm 8:6-8

The Christian's appointed task is threefold. The church's main mandate is evangelism, and every Christian must seek by all means to further the conversion of unbelievers. The impact of one's own changed life will be significant here. Also, neighbor-love should constantly lead the Christian into deeds of mercy of all sorts. In addition, Christians are called to fulfill the "cultural mandate" that God gave to mankind at Creation. Man was made to manage God's world, and this stewardship is part of the human vocation in Christ. It calls for hard work, with God's honor and the good of others as its goal. This is the real "Protestant work ethic." It is essentially a religious discipline, the fulfillment of a divine calling.

Concise Theology, 235-236

REFLECT: God calls Christians to be stewards of God's creation.

God did not send his Son into the world to condemn the world, but to save the world through him.

John 3:17

Society's ways are bad, due to sin, and people need to be rescued from them. Redirecting the misdirected lives of those whom our grandfathers called "precious souls" belongs to the work of evangelism, which is always the first and basic form of social service and the first item of the Christian calling in the secular community. No amount of concern for wider cultural involvements must be allowed to displace evangelism from its priority. Cultural endeavor without evangelism is one stage worse than evangelism without cultural endeavor, for the concentration on evangelism does at least put first things first. But evangelism with cultural endeavor, making common cause with others when they fight for what is right in society, while mounting opposition against them when they go after what is wrong, is the proper formula for fulfilling the Christian's calling in God's world.

"The Christian and God's World," 96

REFLECT: Evangelism and cultural involvement belong together.

As long as it is day, we must do the work of him who sent me. Night is coming, when no one can work. While I am in the world, I am the light of the world.

John 9:4-5

I do not say that discharging the dual mandate of evangelism and cultural endeavor can be made easy or straightforward. I know that in our day, at least, it cannot. The Western societies in which we are called to serve God as his stewards of creation and his Samaritans to those in spiritual and material need are whirling maelstroms of sectional selfishness, economic exploitation, utopian unrealism, crushing collectivism, rival power plays, moral cynicism, and manipulative corner-cutting at every turn. Such conditions are bound constantly to hamper and thwart us, but they must never induce us to stop. It is our business to persist faithfully in our God-given role in the world as the salt that preserves it and the light that guides it, and not to be daunted if our labor feels like a drop in a bucket that makes no difference at all. One day our Master's "Well done" will more than make amends for any discouragements that we may suffer here and now.

"The Christian and God's World," 97

REFLECT: God asks me to persist in the face of discouraging odds.

Show proper respect to everyone:
Love the brotherhood of believers,
fear God, honor the king.

1 Peter 2:17

It is a paradox of the Christian life that the more pro-
foundly one is concerned about heaven, the more deeply one
cares about God's will being done on earth. In the New
Testament, civic obligation is emphatically commanded
alongside—indeed, as part of—the obligation to serve God.
Hence, although Christians are not to think of themselves as
ever at home in this world but rather as sojourning aliens,
Scripture forbids them to be indifferent to the benefits that
flow from good government. Nor, therefore, should they
hesitate to play their part in maximizing these benefits for
others, as well as for themselves. The upholding of stable
government by a law-abiding life, and helping it to fulfill its
role by personal participation where this is possible, is as fitting for us today as it was for Joseph, Moses, David,
Solomon, Nehemiah, Mordecai, and Daniel (to look no further). We must see it as service of God and neighbor.

"How to Recognize a Christian Citizen," insert 4

REFLECT: Scripture commands me to fulfill civic obligations.

God created man in his own image.... God blessed them and said to them, "Be fruitful and increase in number; fill the earth and subdue it. Rule over the fish of the sea and the birds of the air and over every living creature that moves on the ground."

Genesis 1:27-28

Think of all that makes up the world you know—day, night, sky, sea, sun, moon, stars, trees, plants, birds, fish, animals, insects, big things, little things, and most of all yourself and other human beings. Now meet their Maker!—and gauge the excellence of his wisdom and power from the marvelous complexity, order and goodness which you see in his work. And realize too that you, the admiring observer, were made like your Maker in a way that none of these other things are, so that you might manage the lower creation for God, as his steward, and enjoy its riches as his gift to you. That is your calling, so go to it!

"Conscience, Choice and Character," 170

REFLECT: God calls me to enjoy and shape his creation.

God saw all that he had made, and it was very good. And there was evening, and there was morning—the sixth day.

Genesis 1:31

The world exists in its present stable state by the will and power of its Maker. Since it is his world, we are not its owners, free to do as we like with it, but its stewards, answerable to him for the way we handle its resources. And since it is his world, we must not depreciate it. Much religion has built on the idea that the material order—reality as experienced through the body, along with the body that experiences it—is evil, and therefore to be refused and ignored as far as possible. This view, which dehumanizes its devotees, has sometimes called itself Christian, but it is really as un-Christian as can be. For matter, being made by God, was and is *good* in his eyes, and so should be so in ours. We serve God by using and enjoying temporal things gratefully, with a sense of their value to him, their Maker, and of his generosity in giving them to us.

Growing in Christ, 37

REFLECT: The created world is good in God's eyes.

Command those who are rich in this present world not to be arrogant nor to put their hope in wealth, which is so uncertain, but to put their hope in God, who richly provides us with everything for our enjoyment.

1 Timothy 6:17

God gave us all things to enjoy. He willed to be glorified through humanity's learning to appreciate and admire his wisdom and goodness as Creator. In other words, God commissioned mankind to build a culture and civilization. Right at the outset, God introduced Adam to the vocation appointed for him by putting him in charge of a garden. Adam was to learn to see the whole created order as the estate which he, as God's gardener, was responsible for cultivating. Man was not made to be a barbarian, nor to live in savagery, and "back to nature" is never the road back to Eden. For mankind was made to rule nature, to master it, and to enjoy its fruits, to the glory of God the Creator, according to the principle laid down in 1 Timothy 4:4: "Everything God created is good, and nothing is to be rejected if it is received with thanksgiving."

God's Words, 61

REFLECT: God has commissioned mankind to build a civilization.

The LORD God took the man and put him in the Garden of Eden to work it and take care of it.

Genesis 2:15

In the biblical vision, the world belongs to God and we are, at most, his stewards charged to manage God's world for him according to his revealed will. God putting Adam to tend a garden perfectly pictures our God-given cultural mandate. We are to see the entire created order, including, of course, our neighbors and ourselves, as the estate that we, as God's gardeners, are responsible for cultivating. Never forget that the glory of God and the happiness of man were always meant to go together! Where you truly have the former, you will truly have the latter also. It cannot be said too often that this world is in every sense God's world, which his human creatures must learn to handle reverently, for his praise.

"The Christian and God's World," 88

REFLECT: God has made me a steward in charge of his world.

I saw that there is nothing better for a man than to enjoy his work, because that is his lot. For who can bring him to see what will happen after him?

Ecclesiastes 3:22

God made us all for work. Human nature only finds fulfillment and contentment when we have work to do. This appears from the creation story, which tells us that God put Adam "in the Garden of Eden to work it and take care of it" (Genesis 2:15). The work would have required constant thought and effort, as every gardener knows very well; yet it would have been happy partnership with God all the way, ordering the natural life and shaping the spontaneous growth that God gives to trees and plants, and Adam would have perceived himself as fulfilling his human calling to be, in J.R.R. Tolkien's word, a "sub-creator" under God. Had God not required us, made as we are, to work in his world, the experience of fulfillment that these things engender would not be ours. No form of work can guarantee that virtue, love, and joy will become ours, but we need not expect that virtue, love, and joy will ever mark us out if our lives have in them no form of work.

A Passion for Faithfulness, 75-76

REFLECT: God calls me to be a "sub-creator" under him.

We hear that some among you are idle. They are not busy; they are busybodies. Such people we command and urge in the Lord Jesus Christ to settle down and earn the bread they eat.

2 Thessalonians 3:11-12

God has ordained work to be our destiny, both here and hereafter. (Hereafter? Yes, in the heavenly city "his servants will serve him" and "reign for ever and ever" [Revelation 22:3, 5], all of which means active work.) What was his reason for planning our lives this way? I think we see the answer when we note what happens as we work. We then discover our potential as craftsmen, learning to do things and developing skills, which is fascinating. We also discover the potential of God's world as raw material for us to use, manage, and bring into shape, which is fascinating too. If, made as we are, we should become work-shy and give ourselves to pursuing leisure and amusement instead, we should sentence ourselves to deep-level dissatisfaction with life.

A Passion for Faithfulness, 75-76

REFLECT: In work I discover my potential and the potential of God's world.

Whatever you do, work at it with all your heart, as working for the Lord, not for men.

Colossians 3:23

God's command to Adam and Eve to fill and subdue the earth (Genesis 1:28) is sometimes called "the cultural mandate," because every attempt to fulfill it at once produces culture—that is, a pattern of community life based, as all cultures are, on work with a purpose. Work as a way of life that we approve, embrace, and pursue for the glory of God generates within us a spirit of praise to him, both for the wonders of creation outside us and for the creativity that our work draws out of us. Furthermore, work brings joy in the experience of making and managing; work fosters wisdom and maturity in the way we run things, including our relationships with other people (in which also we are meant to be creative); work leads to an increase of affection and goodwill toward others as we harness our skills to serve them; and work develops ingenuity and resourcefulness in finding ways to tap into the powers and processes that surround us.

A Passion for Faithfulness, 75

REFLECT: When I work for the glory of God, I grow in happiness and skill.

Give your servant a discerning heart to govern your people and to distinguish between right and wrong. For who is able to govern this great people of yours?

1 Kings 3:9

Discern what is good and what is bad about the world. God made the cosmic order genuinely good. It is heresy to affirm that the world of matter, physical life, and sensory pleasure is valueless and evil. Down the centuries that heresy has haunted Christian minds and produced many ugly things: a false antithesis between the material and the spiritual; false guilt about enjoying food, physical comfort, and sex in marriage; pride in one's world-denying asceticism; contracting out of the arts and all cultural endeavor; and so on. However, the other side of the truth here is that the world of mankind has become genuinely bad through the moral and spiritual twisting of human nature. The bitter fruit of the fall is that now human relations are disrupted by cruelty, violence, and self-seeking; science is made to serve selfish ambition and the fine arts are used to undermine morality. The created values of human life must not be confused with its acquired corruptions, or we shall never know how to act rightly in God's world.

"The Christian and God's World," 93-94

REFLECT: In a good but fallen world, discernment between good and evil is vital.

You are the salt of the earth.... You are the light of the world.
Matthew 5:13-14

God's first requirement of Christians in this world is that they be different from those around them, observing God's moral absolutes, practicing love, avoiding shameful license, and not losing their dignity as God's image-bearers through any form of irresponsible self-indulgence. A clean break with the world's value systems and lifestyles is called for, as a basis for practicing Christlikeness in positive terms. Then, knowing that God in providential kindness and forbearance continues, in the face of human sin, to preserve and enrich his erring world, Christians are to involve themselves in all forms of lawful human activity, and by doing that in terms of the Christian value system and vision of life they will become salt (a preservative that makes things taste better) and light (an illumination that shows the way to go) in the human community. As Christians thus fulfill their vocation, Christianity becomes a transforming cultural force.

Concise Theology, 235-236

REFLECT: Christians are called to transform the world according to God's value system.

Do not love the world or anything in the world.... For everything in the world—the cravings of sinful man, the lust of his eyes and the boasting of what he has and does—comes not from the Father but from the world. The world and its desires pass away, but the man who does the will of God lives forever.

1 John 2:15-17

People today feel lost. It may seem odd that this is so in an era when we have more control over the forces of nature than ever before, but it really is not: it is God's judgment, which we have brought down on ourselves by trying to feel too much at home in this world. For that is what we have done. We refuse to believe that one should live for something more than this present life. We have treated this world as if it were the only home we shall ever possess and have concentrated exclusively on arranging it for our comfort. We thought we could build heaven on earth, but now God has judged us for our impiety.

Hot Tub Religion, 9-10

REFLECT: This world is not my home.

Do not work for food that spoils, but for food that endures to eternal life, which the Son of Man will give you.

John 6:27

Today, by and large, Christians no longer live for heaven and therefore no longer understand, let alone practice, detachment from the world. Does the world around us seek pleasure, profit, and privilege? So do we. We have no readiness or strength to renounce these objectives, for we have recast Christianity into a mold that stresses happiness above holiness, blessings here above blessedness hereafter, health and wealth as God's best gifts, and death not as thankworthy deliverance from the miseries of a sinful world but as the supreme disaster and a constant challenge to faith in God's goodness. Is our Christianity now out of shape? Yes it is, and the basic reason is that we have lost the New Testament's two-world perspective that views the next life as more important than this one and understands life here as essentially preparation and training for life hereafter. And we shall continue out of shape until this proper other-worldliness is recovered.

Hot Tub Religion, 89-90

REFLECT: Today's Christianity is distorted by emphasis on this world.

Send forth your light and your truth,
let them guide me;
let them bring me to your holy mountain,
to the place where you dwell.
Then will I go to the altar of God,
to God, my joy and my delight.
I will praise you with the harp,
O God, my God.

Psalm 43:3-4

What does Scripture say to us about our pleasures? Does it, as some imagine, tell us to give them all up, as having no place in holy living? Certainly not! Scripture favors pleasure—"I commend the enjoyment of life," says the wise man (Ecclesiastes 8:15)—and only forbids surrender to it as a lifestyle. But this has become an area of real difficulty for Christians in our day. Biblical Christianity does not teach that any pleasure or good feelings, or any form of present ease and contentment, should be sought as life's highest good. What it teaches, rather, is that glorifying God by our worship and service is the true human goal, that rejoicing and delighting in God is central to worship, and that the first fruits of our heritage of pleasures for evermore will be given us as we set ourselves to do this; but should we start to seek pleasure rather than God, we would be in danger of losing both.

"Pleasure Principles," 24-25

REFLECT: Pleasure is an excellent by-product but a bad lifestyle.

Since you died with Christ to the basic principles of this world, why, as though you still belonged to it, do you submit to its rules: "Do not handle! Do not taste! Do not touch!"? Such regulations... lack any value in restraining sensual indulgence.

Colossians 2:20-21, 23

Some regard petitions for personal material needs as low-grade prayer, as if God were not interested in the physical side of life and we should not be either. But such hyper-spirituality is really an unspiritual ego trip; see how Paul warns that man made asceticism does not stop indulgence of the flesh (that is, the sinful self). Petitions looking to God as the sole and omnicompetent source of supply of all human needs, down to the most mundane, are expressing truth, and as the denying of our own self-sufficiency humbles us, so the acknowledging of our dependence honors God. Neither our minds nor our hearts are right till we see that it is as necessary and important to pray for daily bread as for (say) the forgiveness of sins. God really is concerned that his servants should have the food they need, as Jesus' feedings of the four thousand and five thousand show. God cares about physical needs no less than spiritual; to him, the basic category is that of *human* need, comprising both.

Growing in Christ, 187-188

REFLECT: God is concerned about my physical and material needs.

Go, eat your food with gladness,
and drink your wine with a joyful heart,
for it is now that God favors what you do.
Always be clothed in white,
and always anoint your head with oil.

Ecclesiastes 9:7-8

The Christian way is not to deify our bodies, making health and beauty ends in themselves, as modern pagans do; nor is it to despise them, making scruffiness a virtue, as some ancient pagans (and Christians too, unfortunately) once did. It is rather to accept one's body as part of God's good creation, to act as its steward and manager, and gratefully to enjoy it as one does so. Thus we honor its Maker. Such enjoyment is in no way unspiritual for Christ's disciples; for them, it is like their salvation, the Lord's free gift.

The Bible opposes all long-faced asceticism by saying that if you enjoy health, good appetite, physical agility, and marriage in the sense that you have been given them, you should enjoy them in the further sense of delighting in them. Such delight is part of our duty and our service of God, for without it we are being simply ungrateful for good gifts.

Growing in Christ, 188

REFLECT: I honor my Maker when I gratefully enjoy my body as his gift.

A man can do nothing better than to eat and drink and find satisfaction in his work. This too, I see, is from the hand of God, for without him, who can eat or find enjoyment?

Ecclesiastes 2:24-25

A Jewish rabbi suggested that on Judgment Day God would take account of us for neglecting pleasures that he provided. Christian teachers have rightly insisted that contempt for pleasure, so far from arguing superior spirituality, is actually the heresy of Manichaeism and the sin of pride. Pleasure is divinely designed to raise our sense of God's goodness, deepen our gratitude to him, and strengthen our hope of richer pleasures to come in the next world. C. S. Lewis declares that in heaven the highest raptures of earthly lovers will be as milk and water compared with the delights of knowing God. All pleasures are sanctified and, in fact, increased when received and responded to in this way.

Hot Tub Religion, 71

REFLECT: Contempt for pleasure is heresy and sin.

I commend the enjoyment of life, because nothing is better for a man under the sun than to eat and drink and be glad. Then joy will accompany him in his work all the days of the life God has given him under the sun.

Ecclesiastes 8:15

Keeping our heads despite the pull of pleasure is as hard a task as any for the affluent believer. To react by trying to negate pleasure altogether, as if God himself were against it, would be arrogant ingratitude to him; but to retain pleasure in its proper place when all around us seem to have gone pleasure-mad calls for more wisdom than most of us can muster. Let wisdom from Ecclesiastes, the Preacher, instruct us. It is the wisdom that knows that happiness is the spin-off of holiness, the sweet by-product of devotion to God. By taking this wisdom to heart we may learn how to enjoy the pleasures God gives without lapsing into the love of the world. Thus we shall be able to steer a straight course for heaven amid a culture that is obsessively preoccupied with earth.

Hot Tub Religion, 100, 102

REFLECT: Wisdom instructs me to enjoy the pleasures God gives without going pleasure-mad.

The angel said to them, "Do not be afraid. I bring you good news of great joy that will be for all the people."

Luke 2:10

Joy was God's plan for human beings from the beginning. God's purpose that we should enjoy him, both directly in face-to-face fellowship and indirectly through enjoyment of what he has created, is pictured by the fact that the earthly home that he gave Adam and Eve was a pleasure garden where he himself walked in the cool of the day. The New Testament tells us that God "richly provides us with everything for our enjoyment" (1 Timothy 6:17), and that glorified saints endlessly delight in the God whom they endlessly adore. Thus it appears that God's saving activity vindicates, restores, and fulfills his original purpose of joy for man that satanic malice and human sin have thwarted. Joy to the world remains God's goal.

Hot Tub Religion, 138-140

REFLECT: Joy to the world—the Lord is come!

I thought in my heart, "Come now, I will test you with pleasure to find out what is good." But that also proved to be meaningless. "Laughter," I said, "is foolish. And what does pleasure accomplish?"

Ecclesiastes 2:1-2

Joy is not the same thing as fun and games. Many people "have fun," as we say, seeking and finding pleasure, without finding joy. You can "enjoy yourself" and remain joyless. The restless, relentless pursuit of pleasure (sex, drugs, drink, gadgets, entertainment, travel) is very much a mark of our time, at least in the affluent West, and it clearly indicates a lack of joy. Christians who know the joy of the Lord find that a great deal of fun comes with it, but joy is one thing and fun is another. By contrast, Paul in prison had no fun (that seems a safe statement), yet he had much joy. You can have joy without fun, just as you can have fun without joy. There is no necessary connection between the two.

Hot Tub Religion, 150

REFLECT: Pursuing pleasure is not the way to find joy.

Be careful, however, that the exercise of your freedom does not become a stumbling block to the weak.

1 Corinthians 8:9

The privilege of drawing joy from what we know to be our Father's world must be exercised responsibly; otherwise, we sin. Responsible use of freedom limits one's action to what is helpful spiritually to oneself and others. It restricts one to what best serves the glory of God and the good of others, and forbids one to let the merely permissible become the enemy of that best, elbowing it out for the sake of a lesser good. It will often be a more responsible use of freedom to say no to the permissible, just because it would not have a good effect on others, than to say yes to it just in order to make the point that it is indeed permitted under the gospel. Christian liberty must never be swallowed up by subcultural legalism, but neither may it ever degenerate into sub-Christian license. We shall never know how to act rightly in God's world until we are clear on this.

"The Christian and God's World," 95

REFLECT: Joy and responsibility belong together.

"Everything is permissible for me"—but not everything is beneficial. "Everything is permissible for me"—but I will not be mastered by anything.

1 Corinthians 6:12

Worldliness means yielding to the *spirit* that animates fallen mankind, the spirit of self-seeking and self-indulgence without regard for God. Whether a man is worldly thus depends, not on how much enjoyment he takes from the good and pleasant things of this life, but on the spirit in which he takes it. If he allows these things to enslave him and become a god—that is, an idol—in his heart, he is worldly. If, on the other hand, he is disciplined in his use of them, not indulging to the detriment of his own or others' edification nor losing his heart to them, but receiving them gratefully as God's gifts and a means for showing forth his praise, thanking God for all pleasant occupations and all delightful experiences, and not letting the merely good elbow out the best, then he is not worldly but godly.

God's Words, 63-64

REFLECT: Worldliness means being mastered by things that are good in their place.

To the pure, all things are pure, but to those who are corrupted and do not believe, nothing is pure.

Titus 1:15

Look at the motivation and outcome of your pleasures. How hard do you chase after them? What kind of behavior do they produce? What is your response to them when they come? If pleasure comes unsought, or as our grateful acceptance of a gift providentially set before us, and if the pleasure does no damage to ourselves or others, and if the delight of it prompts fresh thanksgiving to God, then it is holy. But if the taking of one's pleasure is a gesture of self-indulgence, pleasing oneself with no concern as to whether one pleases God, then, whether or not the action itself is wasteful or harmful, one has been entrapped by what the Bible sees as the pleasures of the world and of sin. The same pleasant experience—eating, drinking, making love, playing games, listening to music, or whatever—will be good or bad, holy or unholy, depending on how it is handled.

Hot Tub Religion, 70

REFLECT: My attitude can make the difference between godly and worldly pleasure.

Everything God created is good, and nothing is to be rejected if it is received with thanksgiving, because it is consecrated by the word of God and prayer.

1 Timothy 4:4-5

Enslavement to activities is worldliness in its purest form: compulsive workaholism is as worldly as is any form of laziness. Whether persons are worldly or not depends not on how much pleasure they take from life, but on the spirit in which they take it. If we let pleasant things engross us so that we forget God, we are worldly. If we receive them gratefully with a purpose of pleasing God by our appreciation and use of his gifts, we are not worldly but godly. Worldliness is the spirit that substitutes earthly goals (pleasure, profit, popularity, privilege, power) for life's true goal, which is the praise of God.

"The Christian and God's World," 95-96

REFLECT: Worldliness is not pleasure, but confusion of values.

Whether you eat or drink or whatever you do, do it all for the glory of God.

1 Corinthians 10:31

The Bible envisages life as a rhythm of work and rest (generally, labor by day and sleep by night; labor for six days and rest on the seventh) and does not distinguish between spiritual and secular work as if these belonged in two separate compartments. The Bible teaches, rather, that we should plan and live our life as a unity in which nothing is secular and everything is in a real sense sacred, because everything is being done for the glory of God—that is, to show appreciation for what he has made, to please him by loving obedience to his commands, and to advance his honor and praise among his creatures, starting with the homage and adoration that we render to him ourselves. Nothing is to be viewed as less than sacred; there is to be no compartmentalizing of our daily doings; work is to be a unifying reality that holds all our life together.

A Passion for Faithfulness, 74

REFLECT: All of life is sacred when all is done for God's glory.

Be very careful, then, how you live—not as unwise but as wise, making the most of every opportunity, because the days are evil. Therefore do not be foolish, but understand what the Lord's will is.

Ephesians 5:15-17

The underlying principle of the fourth commandment is clear: we must honor God by our use of time, in a rhythm of toil and rest; six days for work crowned by one day for worship. God's claim on our sabbaths reminds us that all our time is his gift, to be given back to him and used for him. That Christians are stewards of the gifts and money that God gives them is a familiar truth nowadays; that we are stewards of the time we are given is less stressed, but just as true. Satan wants to see every minute misused; it is for us to make every minute count for God. How? Not by a frenzied rushing to pack a quart of activity into a pint pot of time (a common present-day error), but by an ordered lifestyle in which, within the set rhythm of toil and rest, work and worship, due time is allotted to sleep, family, wage earning, homemaking, prayer, recreation, and so on, so that we master time instead of being mastered by it.

Growing in Christ, 252-253

REFLECT: Time is God's gift to me, to be used in a rhythm of work and rest.

When the neighboring peoples bring merchandise or grain to sell on the Sabbath, we will not buy from them on the Sabbath or on any holy day. Every seventh year we will forgo working the land and will cancel all debts.

Nehemiah 10:31

The Lord's day is God's gift to us for the health of our souls and of the souls of others, and we must appreciate, honor, and use it accordingly. It is a day of spiritual opportunity, because it is the day of united worship; it is in the worship together of his people that God specially makes himself known. The Puritans, who used to call the Lord's day "the market-day of the soul," the high spot of the week, believed that a well-spent Lord's day was a necessary preparation for the six days' work that would then follow, and that Christians simply could not afford to treat the day as trivial and reduce it to routine. Safeguarding and sanctifying the Lord's day requires of modern Christians ever more clarity of purpose as secularism eats away at Christian public observances and our pagan culture assimilates Sunday more and more completely to being like any other day of the week, thus in effect returning to the paganism of the world to which Christianity first came, and from which Christians were instructed to be distinctively different.

A Passion for Faithfulness, 191

REFLECT: The Lord's day is God's gift for our well-being.

All the people had been weeping as they listened to the words of the Law. Nehemiah said, "Go and enjoy choice food and sweet drinks, and send some to those who have nothing prepared.... Do not grieve, for the joy of the LORD is your strength."

Nehemiah 8:9-10

Weeping! Why? Because of the impact that understanding of God's word was making on their hearts. Grief for sin, and joy in God's forgiveness and the assurance of his love, are not far from each other, for the God who convicts of sin is the God of mercy who saves, and repenting of sin and trusting Christ for forgiveness are two sides of the same coin. This two-sided, double-aspect turning to God is the basic discipline of each day's Christian living, and it is in relation to one or the other facet of it that the most vivid realizings of God, and enlargings of our grip on him, are likely to be given to us. And while there needs to be a time for grief as well as a time for joy, expressing our joy from the Lord can reinforce our spiritual realizations every bit as effectively as expressions of grief can do. Not all service of God need be somber.

A Passion for Faithfulness, 155, 159

REFLECT: Feasting has its place in God's service.

Not to us, O LORD, not to us
but to your name be the glory,
because of your love and faithfulness.

Psalm 115:1

"Man's chief end," says the Shorter Catechism, magnificently, "is to glorify God, and to enjoy him for ever." God has so made us that we find our own deepest fulfillment and highest joy in hallowing his name by praise, submission, and service. God is no sadist, and the principle of our creation is that our duty, interest, and delight completely coincide. Christians get so hung up with the pagan idea (very dishonoring to God, incidentally) that God's will is always unpleasant, so that one is rather a martyr to be doing it, that they hardly at first notice how their experience verifies the truth that in Christian living, duty and delight go together. But they do!—and it will be even clearer in the life to come. To give oneself to hallowing God's name as one's life task means that living, though never a joy ride, will become increasingly a joy *road*. Can you believe that? Well, the proof of the pudding is in the eating! Try it, and you will see.

Growing in Christ, 174

REFLECT: My greatest joy comes when I give glory to God's name by serving him.

AUGUST

God wills us to be holy.

It is God's will that you should be sanctified.

1 Thessalonians 4:3

Holiness is commanded: God wills it, Christ requires it, and all the Scriptures call for it.

Holiness is the goal of our redemption. As Christ died in order that we may be justified, so we are justified in order that we may be sanctified and made holy.

Holiness is the object of our new creation. We are born again so that we may grow up into Christlikeness.

Holiness, as a sign and expression of the reality of one's faith and repentance, and of one's acceptance of God's ultimate purpose, is genuinely necessary for one's final salvation.

Finally, holiness is the substance of which happiness is the spin-off. Those who chase happiness miss it, while to those who pursue holiness through the grace of Christ, happiness of spirit comes unasked.

Rediscovering Holiness, 34-37

REFLECT: God commands me to be holy.

I delight in your commands
because I love them....
They are the joy of my heart.

Psalm 119:47, 111

Holiness starts inside a person, with a right purpose that seeks to express itself in a right performance. It is a matter, not just of the motions that I go through, but of the motives that prompt me to go through them.

A holy person's motivating aim, passion, desire, longing, aspiration, goal, and drive is to please God, both by what one does and by what one avoids doing. In other words, one practices good works and cuts out evil ones. Good works begin with praise, worship, and honoring and exalting God as the temper of one's whole waking life. Evil works start with neglect of these things and coolness with regard to them. So I must labor to keep my heart actively responsive to God.

Rediscovering Holiness, 22

REFLECT: Holiness has to do with my heart.

In Christ Jesus... the only thing that counts is faith expressing itself through love.

Galatians 5:6

Holiness is the demonstration of faith working by love. It is wholly supernatural in the sense of being God's gracious achievement within us, and wholly natural in the sense of being our own true humanness, lost through sin, misconceived through ignorance and through listening too hard to current culture—but now in process of restoration through the redirecting and reintegrating energy of new creation in Christ through the Holy Spirit. Oswald Chambers called holiness "our brilliant heritage." The phrase was well chosen. *Brilliant*—bright, shining, precious, glorious—is the word that fits.

Rediscovering Holiness, 32

REFLECT: Holiness is faith at work through love.

I urge you, brothers, in view of God's mercy, to offer your bodies as living sacrifices, holy and pleasing to God—this is your spiritual act of worship.

Romans 12:1

The holy sacrifice that gives God pleasure is the Christian whose heart never ceases to be grateful to him for his grace. God is pleased with the Christian whose aim every day is to express that gratitude by living to him, through him, and for him, and who is constantly asking, with the psalmist, "How can I repay the LORD for all his goodness to me?" (Psalm 116:12). Such a Christian was the Scottish saint Robert Murray McCheyne, who wrote,

Chosen, not for good in me;
Wakened up from wrath to flee;
Hidden in the Saviour's side,
By the Spirit sanctified;
Teach me, Lord, on earth to show,
By my love, how much I owe.

That is the kind of Christian that I must seek to be.

Rediscovering Holiness, 77

REFLECT: Holiness is expressed in gratitude.

Prepare your minds for action; be self-controlled; set your hope fully on the grace to be given you when Jesus Christ is revealed. Just as he who called you is holy, so be holy in all you do.

1 Peter 1:13, 15

Christian holiness is a number of things together. It is a matter of Spirit-led law-keeping, a walk, or course of life, in the Spirit that displays the fruit of the Spirit (Christlikeness of attitude and disposition). It is a matter of seeking to imitate Jesus' way of behaving, through depending on Jesus for deliverance from carnal self-absorption and for discernment of spiritual needs and possibilities. It is a matter of patient, persistent uprightness; of taking God's side against sin in our own lives and in the lives of others; of worshiping God in the Spirit as one serves him in the world; and of single-minded, wholehearted, free and glad concentration on the business of pleasing God.

Rediscovering Holiness, 31-32

REFLECT: Holiness is the flavor of a life set apart for God that is now being inwardly renewed by his power.

When you spread out your hands in prayer, I will hide my eyes from you; even if you offer many prayers, I will not listen.... Take your evil deeds out of my sight! Stop doing wrong, learn to do right! Seek justice, encourage the oppressed. Defend the cause of the fatherless, plead the case of the widow.

Isaiah 1:15-17

Why should we think personal righteousness important, and make it our daily aim? First, because God commands it. Second, because it pleases him, and gratitude for grace must make us want to please him. Third, because hearty obedience is basic to honest doxology: glorifying God with our lips is hollow and phony unless our lives are right. Fourth, because our own moral transformation gives credibility to our gospel whereas unchanged lives will destroy its credibility. No one will believe what we say about the power of Christ if we ourselves do not show its fruit. Is, then, the moral quality of a Christian's personal life important? Yes, it matters much how we live!

"Does It Really Matter?" 30

REFLECT: Holiness pleases God.

Although [Jesus] was a son, he learned obedience from what he suffered.

Hebrews 5:8

Holiness is something which Christians have to learn in and through experience. As Jesus learned what obedience requires, costs, and involves through the experience of actually doing his Father's will, so Christians must, and do, learn holiness from their battles for purity of heart and righteousness of life.

Talented youngsters who go to tennis school in order to learn the game soon discover that the heart of the process is not talking about tactics but actually practicing serves and strokes, thus forming new habits and reflexes, so as to iron out weaknesses of style. The routine, which is grueling, is one of doing prescribed things over and over again on the court, against a real opponent, in order to get them really right. Holiness is learned in a similar way.

Rediscovering Holiness, 15

REFLECT: Holiness grows through practice.

Good and upright is the LORD;
therefore he instructs sinners in his ways....
All the ways of the LORD are loving and faithful
for those who keep the demands of his covenant.

Psalm 25:8, 10

The process of learning to be holy may properly be thought of as a school—God's own school, in which the curriculum, the teaching staff, the rules, the discipline, the occasional prizes, and the fellow pupils with whom one studies, plays, debates, and fraternizes, are all there under God's sovereign providence.

As pushing ahead on the path of holiness is a prime form of spiritual warfare against sin and Satan, so it is an educational process that God has planned and programmed in order to refine, purge, enlarge, animate, toughen, and mature us. By means of it he brings us progressively into the moral and spiritual shape in which he wants to see us.

Rediscovering Holiness, 16

REFLECT: Holiness is learned through God's educational process.

We are not trying to please men but God, who tests our hearts.
1 Thessalonians 2:4

It is a familiar truth that every Christian's life purpose must be to glorify God. Everything we say and do, all our obedience to God's commands, all our relationships with others, all the use we make of the gifts, talents, and opportunities that God gives us, all our enduring of adverse situations and human hostility, must be so managed as to give God honor and praise for his goodness to those on whom he sets his love. Equally important is the truth that every Christian's full-time employment must be to please God. Jesus did not live to please himself, nor may we. Pleasing God in everything must be our goal. Faith, praise, generosity, obedience to divinely instituted authority, and single-mindedness in Christian service combine to form the prescribed way to do it. God both enables us for this kind of living and takes pleasure in our practice of it. It is his regular procedure in sovereign grace to give what he commands and delight in the result.

Concise Theology, 185-186

REFLECT: My life purpose must be to please God in everything.

Jesus came to them and said, "All authority in heaven and on earth has been given to me."

Matthew 28:18

Authority means dominance, and one recognizes it by submitting to it. Authority is essentially a matter of something or someone being over you, to direct you; authority, in other words, is what you are *under,* and comply with. Whenever we credit anything with authority—a textbook, a ruling, a document, a word from this or that person—we are saying that in its own sphere it is decisive, more or less, as a guide to what we should say and do. And, contrary to much popular belief in these out-of-joint times, acceptance of authentic authority in this way is something natural and gratifying to us; we look for authority outside ourselves because deep down we know we were made for authority relationships, and that being under authentic authority is part of our human fulfillment. We seek true submission to true authority because it is human nature to want it, and real frustration not to find it.

"The Reconstitution of Authority," 3

REFLECT: I obey God because I accept his authority.

Jesus said, "If you hold to my teaching, you are really my disciples. Then you will know the truth, and the truth will set you free... If the Son sets you free, you will be free indeed."

John 8:31-32, 36

Authority is a *teleological* concept, one that relates to the finding and fulfilling of all that is involved in being human. There does not seem ever to have been a time when individuals did not think of their own existence teleologically, in terms of a goal or set of goals, a good life to which the wise person aspires. Nor, it seems, was there ever a time when ideas of moral authority and human fulfillment were not in some way linked together. Whereas the world finds that its idea of freedom as throwing off all external constraints leads only to restless and disillusioned bitterness, Christians know in their bondservice to their Redeemer an inward joy, peace, and contentment. Under the authority of the Father and the Son alone are true freedom and fulfillment found. Under that divine authority the fulfillment that is true freedom, and the freedom that is true fulfillment, become increasingly real for every disciple, and this fact provides a full teleological vindication of the moral authority of God's commands in the gospel.

"The Reconstitution of Authority," 4-5

REFLECT: I find freedom and fulfillment under God's authority.

Because of your stubbornness and your unrepentant heart, you are storing up wrath against yourself for the day of God's wrath, when his righteous judgment will be revealed.

Romans 2:5

Like parents who will not have their children at the table till they have washed their hands, God will not have us at his table—that is, in his fellowship—till our dirt is off. We have to realize that the arrogance, selfishness, meanness, and sheer perversity of our unloving and unlovely lives is to God something impure, offensive, and repellent, and he recoils from it as we do when we are faced with dirt where we had a right to expect cleanliness. If in a restaurant you were offered food on a plate that had obviously not been washed, you would feel disgusted and decline to accept it. Similarly, according to Scripture, our Maker's attitude to persons dominated by the anti-law, anti-God syndrome called sin is one of resolute rejection, "wrath," to be shown forth in "righteous judgment" when the day comes.

Growing in Christ, 115-116

REFLECT: Our holy God is repelled by sin.

Dear friends, I urge you... to abstain from sinful desires, which war against your soul. Live such good lives among the pagans that, though they accuse you of doing wrong, they may see your good deeds and glorify God on the day he visits us.

1 Peter 2:11-12

No statement of Christian orthodoxy should be thought of as complete until it includes a declaration of God's will for human behavior, which is what Christian morality is about. Christian morality is precisely the doctrine of God's commands to mankind, set within the frame of the doctrines of his works for mankind and his ways with mankind. God the Creator, the God of the Bible, wants his human creatures to serve, please, and glorify him by specific types and courses of action that he likes to see, and he directs us accordingly, with sanctions to encourage us to do right and to discourage us from doing wrong. Christian morality, according to Scripture, is a blueprint for living under the authority of this awesomely and intrusively personal Lord, by whose grace we have been saved to serve, and to whom we must one day give account.

"Christian Morality Adrift," 58-59

REFLECT: Christian morality expresses God's will for human behavior.

Thanks be to God that, though you used to be slaves to sin, you wholeheartedly obeyed the form of teaching to which you were entrusted.

Romans 6:17

The practice of Christian morality, which is the outward aspect of living the Christian life, must never be separated in thought, let alone in reality, from the inward aspect of that life—by which I mean such things as the exercise of conscience, the prayers for help, the joy of obedience, the grateful love of God, the active hoping for heaven, the cherishing of a sense of Christ's presence with us, and the constant battling against temptation, depression, apathy, and hardness of heart. In the deepest sense Christian morality—the morality of faith, hope, and love, pursued with discretion, self-control, fair-mindedness and courage—is not Christian at all save as it is made to rest on the truth that Christ's servants live only by being daily forgiven for their daily failures.

"Christian Morality Adrift," 59-60

REFLECT: Christian morality grows out of a heartfelt gratitude for God's forgiveness.

*Against you, you only, have I sinned
and done what is evil in your sight,
so that you are proved right when you speak
and justified when you judge.*

Psalm 51:4

A mature person wants to be recognized as morally responsible for his actions, and as he resents refusal to give him credit for what he says and does right, so he does not refuse blame for saying and doing what he knows was wrong. He is clear that though external factors may have conditioned his action, his own decision was its direct cause—and so, we think, he should be, for that is how it really was. We are repelled by one who says he should not be blamed because he is mentally ill, or society's helpless victim, for however much we incline to say these things about him in extenuation, we know that when he says them about himself he is making excuses and being morally dishonest. To accept accountability for one's choices is part of what it means to be truly human, and any proposal to ignore or change this is not humanizing; just the opposite! It is the most radical and grotesque dehumanization that can be imagined.

"Conscience, Choice and Character," 173

REFLECT: Moral responsibility is part of human dignity.

Do not think that I have come to abolish the Law or the Prophets; I have not come to abolish them but to fulfill them.

Matthew 5:17

God's commands in the natural law, which the Decalogue restates and the New Testament moral teaching embodies, always remain the same in essence, for they are rooted in the realities of creation; although within that basic frame there appear angles, applications, and additions that are determined by the stage that God's gracious covenant purpose for his own needy people has reached at any one time. The law of Christ for his redeemed people should still be seen as meshing with the natural law to supplement its contents, and as focusing the frame of reference within which Christians must pursue the purposes and policies of love and justice that the natural law requires of them. The natural law remains the basis on which all that is distinctive in Christian morality is superimposed.

"Christian Morality Adrift," 64, 68

REFLECT: Christ's law for his redeemed people is rooted in creation.

I tell you the truth, until heaven and earth disappear, not the smallest letter, not the least stroke of a pen, will by any means disappear from the Law until everything is accomplished.

Matthew 5:18

Scripture shows that God intends his law to function in three ways, which Calvin crystallized in classic form for the church's benefit as the law's threefold use. Its first function is *to be a mirror* reflecting to us both the perfect righteousness of God and our own sinfulness and shortcomings. The law is meant to give knowledge of sin and, by showing us our need of pardon and our danger of damnation, to lead us in repentance and faith to Christ. Its second function is *to restrain evil.* Though it cannot change the heart, the law can to some extent inhibit lawlessness by its threats of judgment; thus it secures some civil order and goes some way to protect the righteous from the unjust. Its third function is *to guide the regenerate* into the good works that God has planned for them. The law tells God's children what will please their heavenly Father. The Christian is free from the law as a supposed system of salvation, but is under Christ's law (Galatians 6:2) as a rule of life.

Concise Theology, 94-95

REFLECT: God's law will not save me, but it can instruct, warn, and guide me.

My son, do not forget my teaching,
but keep my commands in your heart,
for they will prolong your life many years
and bring you prosperity.

Proverbs 3:1-2

The blueprint for this life was set out for all time in the Ten Commandments, which God gave the Jews through Moses on Sinai about thirteen centuries before Christ. Today's world, even today's church, has largely forgotten them (could you recite them?). That is our folly and loss. For here, in nugget form, is the wisdom we need.

Because Scripture calls God's Ten Commandments "law," we assume they are like the law of the land, restricting personal freedom for the sake of public order. But the comparison is wrong. *Torah* (Hebrew for "law") means the sort of instruction a good parent gives his child. God's law exists, not to thwart self-expression (though it may sometimes feel like that—for children hate discipline!), but to lead us into those ways that are best for us.

Growing in Christ, 223-224

REFLECT: God's parental law expresses God's parental love.

This is how we know that we love the children of God: by loving God and carrying out his commands.

1 John 5:2

Love is to be directed by law. God our Maker and Redeemer has revealed the unchanging pattern of response that he requires, and that man needs if he is to be truly himself. The pattern is both an expression of God's own moral character—an indication of what he approves and disapproves—and a clue to man about his own nature and that of his neighbor. By adhering to the pattern, we express and further our own true humanness on the one hand and true love for our neighbor on the other. Our fellow man is always something of an enigma to ourselves, but our Maker, who knows our true nature and needs, has told us how we are to do ourselves and each other real good. So love and law-keeping are mutually entailed.

"Situations and Principles," 163

REFLECT: Love is guided by God's law.

The commandments, "Do not commit adultery," "Do not murder," "Do not steal," "Do not covet," and whatever other commandment there may be, are summed up in this one rule: "Love your neighbor as yourself." Love does no harm to its neighbor. Therefore love is the fulfillment of the law.

Romans 13:9-10

The Ten Commandments' stock is low today. Why? Partly because they are law, naming particular things that should and should not be done. People dislike law (that is one sign of our sinfulness), and the idea is widespread that Christians should not be led by law, only by love. But the love-or-law antithesis is false. Love and law are not opponents but allies, forming together the axis of true morality. Law needs love as its drive, else we get the Pharisaism that puts principles before people and says one can be perfectly good without actually loving one's neighbor. And love needs law as its eyes, for love (Christian *agape* as well as sexual *eros*) is blind. To want to love someone Christianly does not of itself tell you how to do it. Only as we observe the limits set by God's law can we really do people good.

Growing in Christ, 231-232

REFLECT: Love and law are allies.

There is a way that seems right to a man,
but in the end it leads to death.

Proverbs 14:12

Situationism is worldliness, not only because it opens the door to wayward self-indulgence, but also because it aims to squeeze Christian morality into the fashionable "permissive" mold of decadent Western secularism, which rejects the restrictions of all external authority and is sure that we are wise and good enough to see what is really best just by looking. But by biblical standards this is one of many delusions born of the satanic, God-defying pride with which we fallen creatures are all infected.

Moral permissiveness, supposedly so liberating and fulfilling, is actually wounding and destructive: not only of society (which God's law protects), but also of the lawless individual, who gets coarsened and reduced as a person every time. The first advocate of permissiveness was Satan at the Fall, but his promise of God-likeness to the lawless was a lie. The Christian's most loving service to his neighbor in our modern world, which so readily swallows this ancient lie, is to uphold the authority of God's law as man's one true guide to true life.

Growing in Christ, 232-233

REFLECT: Moral permissiveness hurts people.

Go and learn what this means: "I desire mercy, not sacrifice."
For I have not come to call the righteous, but sinners.

Matthew 9:13

If our thoughts about doing God's will get detached from our thoughts about the inner spiritual life, as if these were two areas of reality and not one, or if—even worse—we define the Christian life entirely in terms of external obedience and forget that there is more to it than mechanically correct performance, then we can hardly avoid ending up in some version of legalistic Pharisaism, in which all the emphasis is on what we do rather than what we are, and into which the reality of Christian freedom does not enter. Then, like the Jews of Paul's day, we shall be rightly accused of going around to establish our own works-righteousness, and of lacking proper acquaintance with the Christ whose saving grace is for sinners only.

"Christian Morality Adrift," 59

REFLECT: The Christian life is more than law-keeping.

Woe to you, teachers of the law and Pharisees, you hypocrites! You are like whitewashed tombs, which look beautiful on the outside but on the inside are full of dead men's bones and everything unclean.

Matthew 23:27

Asceticism, as such—voluntary abstinences, routines of self-deprivation, and grueling austerity—is not the same thing as holiness, though some forms of asceticism may well find a place in a holy person's life. Nor is formalism, in the sense of outward conformity in word and deed to the standards God has set, anything like holiness, though assuredly there is no holiness without such conformity. Nor is legalism, in the sense of doing things to earn God's favor or to earn more of it than one has already, to be regarded as holiness. The Pharisees of Jesus' day made all three mistakes yet were thought to be very holy people until Jesus told them the truth about themselves and the inadequacies of their supposed piety. After that, we dare not forget that holiness begins in the heart.

Rediscovering Holiness, 23

REFLECT: Holiness is not gained by asceticism, formalism, or legalism.

We are God's workmanship, created in Christ Jesus to do good works, which God prepared in advance for us to do.

Ephesians 2:10

"Good works" must be good not only in their content but also in the manner in which they are done and the motive with which we do them. The legalistic formalism of the Pharisees concentrated on matter but ignored manner and motive. True holiness requires that the motive be twofold: the glory of God through the expressing of gratitude for grace, and the good of our fellow men through the service of their needs. Holiness requires also that the manner should be appropriate to the matter; in other words, that we should do each thing, as we say, "properly." Our awareness that this is so should make us realize that we can never hope to do anything right, never expect to perform a work that is truly good, unless God works within us to make us will and act for his good pleasure. Realizing this will make us depend constantly on our indwelling Lord, which is the heart of what is meant by abiding in Christ.

Hot Tub Religion, 192

REFLECT: My good works grow out of God's working within me.

Praise be to the name of God for ever and ever;
wisdom and power are his.

Daniel 2:20

Wisdom in Scripture means choosing the best and noblest end at which to aim, along with the most appropriate and effective means to it. The outworking of God's wisdom involves the expression of his will in two senses. In the first and fundamental sense, God's will is his decision, or decree, about what shall happen. This is God's will of *events*. In the second and secondary sense, the will of God is his command, that is, his instruction, given in Scripture, as to how people should and should not behave. This is sometimes called his will of *precept*. It is sometimes hard to believe that costly obedience, putting us at a disadvantage in the world (as loyal obedience to God often does) is part of a predestined plan for furthering both God's glory and our own good. But we are to glorify God by believing that it is so, and that one day we shall see it to be so; for his wisdom is supreme and never fails.

Concise Theology, 48-49

REFLECT: When I obey God, I help fulfill his will.

*"This is the covenant I will make with the house of Israel
after that time," declares the LORD.
"I will put my law in their minds
and write it on their hearts.
I will be their God,
and they will be my people."*

Jeremiah 31:33

The Spirit continues writing God's law on our hearts all
our lives, as he instructs us from Scripture in God's standards
and makes us judge how far we yet fall short of the moral and
spiritual perfection which they embody. In his letters Paul not
only teaches Christians about Christ and the Spirit, but in the
second half he regularly drills them in ethics—that is, in the
law as it applies to believers. It would be hazardous to try to
be wiser than Paul in our way of teaching the Christian life. If
we remember that as Christians we serve God not for life but
from life, as his already justified and adopted sons and daugh-
ters, we shall not fall into the legalism which some teachers
fear; rather, we shall see God's law as the family code, and it
will be our joy to try to live up to it and so please our heavenly Father who loved and saved us.

God's Words, 105

REFLECT: A child of God finds joy in living by the family
code.

Moses summoned all Israel and said: Hear, O Israel, the decrees and laws I declare in your hearing today. Learn them and be sure to follow them.

Deuteronomy 5:1

Man was not created autonomous, that is, free to be a law unto himself, but theonomous, that is, bound to keep the law of his Maker. This was no hardship, for God had so constructed him that grateful obedience would have brought him highest happiness; duty and delight would have coincided, as they did in Jesus. The fallen human heart dislikes God's law, both because it is a law and because it is God's. Those who know Christ, however, find not only that they love the law and want to keep it, out of gratitude for grace, but also that the Holy Spirit leads them into a degree of obedience, starting with the heart, that was never theirs before.

Concise Theology, 91

REFLECT: I am happiest when the Holy Spirit helps me to obey God's law.

The people went out and brought back branches and built themselves booths... and lived in them. From the days of Joshua son of Nun until that day, the Israelites had not celebrated it like this. And their joy was very great.

Nehemiah 8:16-17

The effort and, no doubt, inconvenience of collecting tree branches from all over, erecting shanties in Jerusalem wherever there was space to do so, and living in them for the festival week was taken in stride; the joy of obedience and of knowing that this pleased God carried all before it. This was spiritual reality! This was life worth living! Nothing compares with knowing that you are doing God's will! Thus the people felt, and they acted accordingly. Here is a pattern of spiritual life that is as authentic today as it was in the time of Ezra and Nehemiah two and a half millennia ago. When a person finds new life in Jesus Christ, and when a drooping Christian undergoes any form of quickening or renewal, obeying God ceases to be a drudgery and becomes a delight, and pleasing God by doing what he asks becomes the chief joy of life.

A Passion for Faithfulness, 159-160

REFLECT: The joy of pleasing God makes life worth living.

I have told you this so that my joy may be in you and that your joy may be complete.

John 15:11

Christianity views mankind as made for delight, but by reason of our fallenness missing it. Joy is never the habitual experience of those who are not right with God. Shelley, himself an unbeliever, testified on behalf of all such when he said, "Rarely, rarely comest thou, Spirit of delight." For God has sovereignly linked happiness with holiness and sin with misery, and to break these links is beyond our power. Only as life becomes love and worship of God, and love and service of our neighbor, in the knowledge of sins forgiven and heaven to come, does joy become unqualified and unending for us, as by Jesus' own testimony it was for him. Knowing God brings joy that grows.

"A Christian View of Man," 113-114

REFLECT: Happiness and holiness are linked.

You need to persevere so that when you have done the will of God, you will receive what he has promised.

Hebrews 10:36

Biblical Christianity, speaking from its unashamedly otherworldly standpoint from which it sees this life as the journey home and the future life as home itself, proclaims the vision, adoration, and enjoyment of God, in perfect righteousness with fullness of joy and love, as the true end of man. Now if worship and godliness were not integral to our happiness, the moral authority of God's summons to both would be in question, for commands whose fulfillment goes against the well-being of those commanded are to that extent morally disreputable. But the Christian claim is that because of the way we are made, the more wholeheartedly and thankfully we submit to God's authority, the deeper will be the personal fulfillment into which we come. Thus, under the gospel, duty and interest coincide. In heaven our fulfillment will be complete, partly because there our acceptance of God's authority will be complete too. Here on earth we are called to move toward that goal as far and as fast as we can, by doing the will of God from our hearts.

"The Reconstitution of Authority," 4

REFLECT: I find fulfillment as I do God's will.

I have been crucified with Christ and I no longer live, but Christ lives in me. The life I live in the body, I live by faith in the Son of God, who loved me and gave himself for me.

Galatians 2:20

In the superb covenant service of the Methodist church, the worshipers join in words which John Wesley took from the Puritan Richard Alleine for this purpose in 1755:

"I am no longer my own, but Thine. Put me to what Thou wilt, rank me with whom Thou wilt; put me to doing, put me to suffering; let me be employed for Thee or laid aside for Thee, exalted for Thee or brought low for Thee; let me be full, let me be empty; let me have all things, let me have nothing; I freely and heartily yield all things to Thy pleasure and disposal.

"And now, O glorious and blessed God, Father, Son and Holy Spirit, Thou art mine, and I am Thine. So be it. And the Covenant which I have made on earth, let it be ratified in heaven. Amen."

Growing in Christ, 181

REFLECT: Am I ready to make this covenant prayer my own?

SEPTEMBER

God wills us to
be Christlike.

No one can come to me unless the Father who sent me draws him, and I will raise him up at the last day.

John 6:44

God works in people's hearts by sovereign grace, taking away their imperviousness to his word, taking away their inability to respond to that word, and changing the disposition of their hearts so that instead of saying "Nonsense" when they hear the word of Christ, they say, "That's just what I need." And they come.

Are you a Christian? A believer? Then you came to Christ because you found yourself willing, longing, desirous, wanting to, as well as, perhaps, not wanting to but knowing you must. How was that? It was because God worked in your heart to give you this desire. He changed you. It was his irresistible grace that drew you to the Savior's feet. Praise him for it! It was one expression of his love to you.

"To All Who Will Come," 184-185

REFLECT: God's grace draws me to Christ.

In him we were also chosen, having been predestined according to the plan of him who works out everything in conformity with the purpose of his will, in order that we, who were the first to hope in Christ, might be for the praise of his glory.

Ephesians 1:11-12

Predestination is a word often used to signify God's fore-ordaining of all the events of world history, past, present, and future, and this usage is quite appropriate. In Scripture, however, predestination means specifically God's decision, made in eternity before the world and its inhabitants existed, regarding the final destiny of individual sinners. In fact, the New Testament uses the words *predestination* and *election* only of God's choice of particular sinners for salvation and eternal life. Sinners choose Christ only because God chose them for this choice and moved them to it by renewing their hearts. Though all human acts are free in the sense of being self-determined, none are free from God's control according to his eternal purpose and foreordination. Christians should therefore thank God for their conversion, look to him to keep them in the grace into which he has brought them, and confidently await his final triumph, according to his plan.

Concise Theology, 38-39

REFLECT: I choose Christ because God chose me.

When he, the Spirit of truth, comes, he will guide you into all truth. He will not speak on his own; he will speak only what he hears, and he will tell you what is yet to come. He will bring glory to me by taking from what is mine and making it known to you.

John 16:13-14

Through the Holy Spirit's work in people's hearts, they become certain that Jesus Christ lives to save those who turn from sin to be his; and that there is no salvation save through personal trust in him. So they actively and deliberately commit themselves to him, not only because they know they need to, but because they find themselves so changed that they want to. For some, this commitment occurs as a clear and conscious break with an unconverted past. For others, it emerges as a focusing of what has been implicit in their life for some time, perhaps from infancy. One way or another, out of changed hearts there issues a commitment to live changed lives, while the Spirit within us witnesses both to Jesus' reality, as the mighty Savior who is there for us, and to our own renewal, as penitent sinners who have now made him the object of our wholehearted loyalty.

Rediscovering Holiness, 54

REFLECT: The Holy Spirit leads me to commit myself to Jesus Christ.

When the people heard this, they were cut to the heart and said to Peter and the other apostles, "Brothers, what shall we do?" Peter replied, "Repent and be baptized, every one of you, in the name of Jesus Christ for the forgiveness of your sins. And you will receive the gift of the Holy Spirit."

Acts 2:37-38

When Peter, preaching at Pentecost, told the Jews that the man they murdered was risen and reigning, many were flabbergasted and asked what they ought to do. It is easy to miss the full force of Peter's answer. Peter was prescribing not a formal gesture of regret for the crucifixion, but total renunciation of independence as a way of living and total submission to the rule of the risen Lord. For Jesus' name carries Jesus' claim, and undergoing baptism is a sign that the claim is being accepted. Everyone baptized in Jesus' name must become Jesus' follower.

Growing in Christ, 111-112

REFLECT: To be baptized in Jesus' name means to submit to Jesus as Lord.

We, who with unveiled faces all reflect the Lord's glory, are being transformed into his likeness with ever-increasing glory, which comes from the Lord, who is the Spirit.

2 Corinthians 3:18

In Christ believers are involved in a process of character change. The Holy Spirit and Christ now indwell them to transform them into Christ's likeness. Christ and his Spirit empower them to put sinful habits to death and bring forth in them the new behavior patterns that constitute the Spirit's "fruit" (see Galatians 5:22-26). This is momentous. We who believe have to wake up to the fact that the ministry to us of the Father and the Son through the Spirit has turned us into different people from what we were by nature. Our present task is to be what we are—to live out what God has wrought in us, expressing in action the new life (new vision, motivation, devotion, and sense of direction) that has now become ours. Or, as Paul puts it, "Live a life worthy of the calling you have received" (Ephesians 4:1).

Rediscovering Holiness, 55

REFLECT: The Holy Spirit calls me to live like Christ.

If anyone is in Christ, he is a new creation; the old has gone, the new has come!

2 Corinthians 5:17

Union with Christ is a creative act on God's part. It is mysterious in character, for it is a fresh putting forth of the power that raised Jesus from the dead. The risen Jesus is at present out of our sight, and neither his life nor that which Christians enjoy in union with him is open to human inspection. But this vitalizing union with Christ is none the less real for being mysterious, as appears from its transforming effects. Union with Christ in his death means, first, that our guilt is gone; second, that our former life under the rule of sin is gone, and a new life of fellowship with Christ has begun. Resurrection with Christ means effective deliverance from slavery to sin to live in the Spirit, being conformed to Christ ever more thoroughly in mind and heart, attitude and outlook. By his Spirit, Christ himself is not merely with us but in us. This is what union with Christ means.

"The Holy Spirit and the Local Congregation," 103

REFLECT: As a Christian, I am united with Christ.

We were... buried with him through baptism into death in order that, just as Christ was raised from the dead through the glory of the Father, we too may live a new life. If we have been united with him like this in his death, we will certainly also be united with him in his resurrection.

Romans 6:4-5

God's eternal Son became Jesus the Christ by incarnation; to put away our sins he tasted death by crucifixion; he resumed bodily life for all eternity by resurrection; and he reentered heaven's glory by ascension. This is what theologians sometimes call the *Christ-event.* It is truly historical, for it happened in Palestine 2,000 years ago. Equally true, however, it is trans-historical, in the sense of not being bounded by space and time as other events are: it can touch and involve in itself any person at any time anywhere. Faith in Jesus occasions that involving touch, so that in terms of rock-bottom reality every believer has actually died and risen, and now lives and reigns, with Jesus and through Jesus. In the Jesus to whom we go in faith, the power of the whole Christ-event resides, and in saving us he not only sets us right with God, but also, so to speak, plugs us in to his own dying, rising, and reigning. Thus we live in joyful fellowship with him.

Growing in Christ, 120

REFLECT: United with Christ, I have died to sin and been raised to new life.

It is by grace you have been saved, through faith—and this not from yourselves, it is the gift of God—not by works, so that no one can boast.

Ephesians 2:8-9

The widespread idea that Christianity celebrates the value of the individual by affirming his natural goodness and then teaching him how to do even better is false. Christianity diagnoses the individual as morally distorted and spiritually ruined, and against that dark background points to Christ as the only one who can straighten out our twisted natures. I am saying that Jesus Christ remakes us in his own moral and spiritual image, and that this is something which we cannot do for ourselves by our own resources. I am further saying, therefore, that at some point each of us must admit that we need to be saved, since we cannot save ourselves. We have not got what it takes to reorder our disordered lives; we need to be saved by Jesus Christ. It is those who in humble honesty reach that moment of truth who become Christians.

"A Christian View of Man," 118

REFLECT: Only Christ can straighten out my twisted nature.

It is for freedom that Christ has set us free. Stand firm, then, and do not let yourselves be burdened again by a yoke of slavery.
Galatians 5:1

The world assumes that the essence of freedom is to be free *from* this or that external pressure: poverty, race prejudice, economic exploitation, political injustice, and the like. But that is only freedom's outward shell; it is not the real thing. The essence of true freedom is being free *for* what matters most—free, that is, for God and godliness, and so for the delight which grace and godliness together bring. The only way into that freedom, however, is to be set free from the egocentricity which binds us by nature, and that is something which Jesus Christ himself alone can do.

"A Christian View of Man," 115

REFLECT: Jesus is the only source of true freedom.

The heart is deceitful above all things
and beyond cure.
Who can understand it?

Jeremiah 17:9

Free will has been defined by Christian teachers as the ability to choose all the moral options that a situation offers, and original sin has robbed us of free will in this sense. We have no natural ability to discern and choose God's way because we have no natural inclination Godward; our hearts are in bondage to sin, and only the grace of regeneration can free us from that slavery. This was what Paul taught in Romans 6:16-23; only the *freed* will freely and heartily chooses righteousness. A permanent love of righteousness—that is, an inclination of heart to the way of living that pleases God—is one aspect of the freedom that Christ gives. I am a morally responsible free agent, but I am also the slave of sin whom Christ must liberate. I am a fallen being and only have it in me to choose against God until God renews my heart.

Concise Theology, 86

REFLECT: Only in Christ am I free to choose God's will.

Do not do what they do, for they do not practice what they preach. They tie up heavy loads and put them on men's shoulders, but they themselves are not willing to lift a finger to move them.

Matthew 23:3-4

Legalism is a distortion of obedience that can never produce truly good works. Its first fault is that it skews motive and purpose, seeing good deeds as essentially ways to earn more of God's favor than one has at the moment. Its second fault is arrogance. Belief that one's labor earns God's favor begets contempt for those who do not labor in the same way. Its third fault is lovelessness in that its self-advancing purpose squeezes humble kindness and creative compassion out of the heart. Legalism puts our relationship with God in jeopardy and, by stopping us focusing on Christ, it starves our souls while feeding our pride. Legalistic religion in all its forms should be avoided like the plague.

Concise Theology, 176-177

REFLECT: I must look to Christ, not to myself, for God's favor.

For this reason he had to be made like his brothers in every way, in order that he might become a merciful and faithful high priest in service to God, and that he might make atonement for the sins of the people.

Hebrews 2:17

It cannot be said too strongly or too often that, for Christians, Jesus is both the model and the means of true and total humanness in a world where our own human nature has in every case been distorted and diminished by sin. Incarnation means that Jesus, who was one hundred percent divine, was also one hundred percent human, and it is supremely by observing his divine humanity that we learn what constitutes full and authentic humanness for ourselves. In Jesus we see what humanity is meant to be and what through Jesus' own mediation our flawed humanity may become.

"A Christian View of Man," 111

REFLECT: Jesus is the model of true humanity.

You have taken off your old self with its practices and have put on the new self, which is being renewed in knowledge in the image of its Creator.

Colossians 3:9-10

North American culture effectively lost God two generations ago; now, by inevitable consequence, it is in the process of losing man. What does it mean to be truly and fully human? The post-Christian world around us no longer knows, and is being sucked down into deep cultural decadence for lack of this knowledge. Biblical Christianity, however, still has the answer, if anyone is still willing to listen. The Bible proclaims that humanness is more than just having a mind and a body; it is essentially a personal and relational ideal, the ideal of living in the image of God, which means being like Jesus Christ in creative love and service to our Father in heaven and our fellow men on earth.

"An Introduction to Systematic Spirituality," 3-4

REFLECT: Only as I live like Jesus am I truly human.

We proclaim [Christ], admonishing and teaching everyone with all wisdom, so that we may present everyone perfect in Christ.

Colossians 1:28

Holiness has to do with my humanness.

Genuine holiness is genuine Christlikeness, and genuine Christlikeness is genuine humanness—the only genuine humanness there is. Love in the service of God and others, humility and meekness under the divine hand, integrity of behavior expressing integration of character, wisdom with faithfulness, boldness with prayerfulness, sorrow at people's sins, joy at the Father's goodness, and single-mindedness in seeking to please the Father morning, noon, and night, were all qualities seen in Christ, the perfect man.

Christians are meant to become human as Jesus was human. We are called to imitate these character qualities, with the help of the Holy Spirit, so that the childish instability, inconsiderate self-seeking, pious play-acting, and undiscerning pigheadedness that so frequently mar our professedly Christian lives are left behind. The beauty of holiness is the beauty of truly mature humanity. I need to remember this, and take it to heart, and set my sights accordingly.

Rediscovering Holiness, 28-29

REFLECT: Genuine Christlikeness is genuine humanness.

Whoever serves me must follow me; and where I am, my servant also will be. My Father will honor the one who serves me.

John 12:26

In God's school of holiness our Lord Jesus Christ is with us, and we with him, in a controlling relationship of master and servant, leader and follower, teacher and student. It is crucially important to appreciate this. Why is it that in the school of holiness some move ahead faster than others? Fundamentally, the factor that makes the difference is neither one's intelligence quotient nor the number of books one has read nor the conferences, camps, and seminars one has attended, but the quality of the fellowship with Christ that one maintains through life's vicissitudes.

Jesus is risen. He is alive and well. Through his word and Spirit he calls us to himself today, to receive him as our Savior and Lord and become his disciples and followers.

Rediscovering Holiness, 17

REFLECT: My progress in the school of holiness depends on my relationship with Jesus Christ, my teacher.

My God will meet all your needs according to his glorious riches in Christ Jesus.

Philippians 4:19

What do we sinners need for a right and good relationship with God? First, we are ignorant of him and need instruction—for no satisfying relationship is possible with a person about whom you know little or nothing. Second, we are estranged from him and need reconciliation—otherwise we shall end up unaccepted, unforgiven, and unblessed, strangers to his fatherly love and exiles from the inheritance which is in store for those who are his children. Third, we are weak, blind, and foolish when it comes to the business of living for God, and we need someone to guide, protect, and strengthen us. In the person and ministry of the one man, Jesus Christ, this threefold need is completely and perfectly met! Hallelujah!

Growing in Christ, 40

REFLECT: Jesus meets my need for a good relationship with God.

God, who said, "Let light shine out of darkness," made his light shine in our hearts to give us the light of the knowledge of the glory of God in the face of Christ.

2 Corinthians 4:6

We need to remember that growth which comes from God through the means of grace (Bible truth, prayer, worship, and fellowship) comes only as in using them we look beyond them to the Lord himself, asking him to bless for our spiritual welfare what we are doing. This is what it really means to grow in grace—that you have your eyes on the Lord and your hope in the Lord all the time, and so are coming constantly to know him better. Real growth in grace will bring you consciously closer to Jesus Christ day by day, and that indeed will be one of the signs that God really is at work in your life. As you see him more clearly, love him more dearly, and follow him more nearly, you will grow in the knowledge of your Savior, sin-bearer, example, master, and source of all the strength and power you need to follow in his steps.

"The Means of Growth," 10-11

REFLECT: When God is at work in my life, I grow ever closer to Jesus.

Grace and peace be yours in abundance through the knowledge of God and of Jesus our Lord. His divine power has given us everything we need for life and godliness through our knowledge of him who called us by his own glory and goodness.

2 Peter 1:2-3

Structurally, God's image in us is a natural given fact, consisting of the rational powers of the human self, as such. Substantively, however, God's image in us is an ongoing moral process, the fruit and expression of a supernatural character change from self-centeredness to God-centeredness and from acquisitive pride to outgoing love—a change that only Christians undergo. So the conclusion of the matter is that the true and full image of God is precisely godliness—communion with God, and creativity under God, in the relational rationality and righteousness that spring from faith, and gratitude to one's Savior, and the desire to please and honor God and to be a means of helping others. The true goal of life is to know and receive and cooperate with God's grace in Christ, through which our potential for Christlikeness may be realized.

"An Introduction to Systematic Spirituality," 4

REFLECT: Living in God's image means becoming Christlike.

Come to me, all you who are weary and burdened, and I will give you rest.

Matthew 11:28

"Going to Jesus" is an umbrella phrase that covers three things:

- praying;
- meditating: thinking, reflecting, drawing conclusions from Scripture, and applying them directly to oneself in Jesus' presence;
- holding oneself open throughout the process to specific illumination from the Holy Spirit.

Christians who go to Jesus cope with events in a spirit of peace, joy, and eagerness to see what God will do next. Others, however, who are no less committed to Jesus as their Savior, never master this art of habitually going to him about life's challenges. Too often they start by assuming that their life as children of God will be a bed of roses all the way. Then when the storms come, the best they can do is stagger through in a spirit of disappointment with God.

It is easy to understand why those who go to Jesus advance farther and faster in the love, humility, and hope that form the essence of Christlike holiness than those who neglect going to him.

Rediscovering Holiness, 18-19

REFLECT: Jesus asks me to take all my concerns to him.

He is the image of the invisible God, the firstborn over all creation.

Colossians 1:15

Praying to God is a problem for many today. Some go through the motions with no idea why; some have exchanged prayer for quiet thought or transcendental meditation; most, perhaps, have given prayer up entirely. Why the problem? The answer is clear. People feel a problem about prayer because of the muddle they are in about God. If you are uncertain whether God exists, or whether he is personal, or good, or in control of things, or concerned about ordinary folk like you and me, you are bound to conclude that praying is pretty pointless, not to say trivial, and then you won't do it.

But if you believe that Jesus is the image of God—in other words, that God is Jesus-like in character—then you will have no such doubts, and you will recognize that for us to speak to the Father and the Son in prayer is as natural as it was for Jesus to talk to his Father in heaven, or for the disciples to talk to their Master during the days of his earthly ministry.

Growing in Christ, 155

REFLECT: Jesus links me to God in prayer.

Be filled with the Spirit. Speak to one another with psalms, hymns, and spiritual songs. Sing and make music in your heart to the Lord, always giving thanks to God the Father for everything, in the name of our Lord Jesus Christ.

Ephesians 5:18-20

There is no holiness without a Christ-centered, Christ-seeking, Christ-serving, Christ-adoring heart. The plan of salvation requires us to get our hearts into this frame and keep them there. How can we do that? It is far more easily said than done!

One help is to think often about the cross. Another is to soak one's soul constantly in the four Gospels, where the majesty and beauty of Jesus are projected with electrifying power. A third help is use of a good hymnbook in one's personal prayers, alongside God's own hymnbook, the Psalms.

In the hymnbooks I know, up to half the songs express praise and love for Jesus in an explicit way. Weaving them into my prayers moves my heart in the desired direction. Love of great hymns—especially those of the two Wesleys, Isaac Watts, and John Newton—has many good effects, and the zeal for the glory of Christ that you catch from them is one of the best helps to holiness that I know.

Rediscovering Holiness, 81-82

REFLECT: Praising Jesus helps me live a holy life.

We ought always to thank God for you, brothers, and rightly so, because your faith is growing more and more, and the love every one of you has for each other is increasing.

2 Thessalonians 1:3

Growth in grace means an increase in the spirit of loving, whereby you care for others and actually lay out your time, trouble, strength, prayers, and every other resource to help them. The Lord is our model here. This was the kind of ministry he had throughout. He ever lived in terms of the principle that it is God first, others second, oneself last. Even on the cross, in his final agony, he was still concerned for others. When they nailed him to the cross he prayed for the soldiers who were doing it. As he hung on the cross he saw his mother and told John to look after her. When the penitent thief spoke to him he said, "Today you will be with me in paradise" (Luke 23:43). This was love—self-giving to the uttermost.

"The Means of Growth," 9

REFLECT: Jesus is my model of self-giving love.

Whatever you do, whether in word or deed, do it all in the name of the Lord Jesus, giving thanks to God the Father through him.
Colossians 3:17

Some who trust Jesus as their Savior have formed the habit of going to him about everything that comes up, in order to become clear on how they should react to it as his disciples. These Christians

- consecrate themselves totally to the Father, as Jesus did;
- say and do only what pleases the Father, as Jesus did;
- accept pain, grief, disloyalty, and betrayal, as Jesus did;
- care for people without compromise of principle or ulterior motives in practice, as Jesus did;
- accept opposition and isolation, hoping patiently for better things and meantime staying steady under pressure, as Jesus did;
- rejoice in the specifics of the Father's ways and thank him for his wisdom and goodness, as Jesus did.

Rediscovering Holiness, 18

REFLECT: God is calling me to live as Jesus did.

Heal the sick who are there and tell them, "The kingdom of God is near you."

Luke 10:9

God's kingdom is not a place, but rather a relationship. It exists wherever people enthrone Jesus as lord of their lives. When Jesus began preaching that "the kingdom of God is near," he meant that the long-promised enjoyment of God's salvation for which Israel had been waiting was now there for them to enter into (Mark 1:15). How were they to enter it? The Gospels answer that question very fully. Why, by becoming Jesus' disciples; by giving him their hearts' loyalty and letting him reshape their lives; by receiving forgiveness from him; by identifying with his concerns; by loving him without reserve and giving his claims precedence over all others. None of us can enter the kingdom without the Spirit's help, and we must not be too proud to ask for it, nor refuse to be changed in whatever ways God sees necessary.

Growing in Christ, 176

REFLECT: When I am in God's kingdom, I live as Jesus' disciple.

I thank Christ Jesus our Lord, who has given me strength, that he considered me faithful, appointing me to his service.

1 Timothy 1:12

Know yourself as a servant of Christ. Remember that you are absolutely at his beck and call. That is your identity as Christ's saved one. That is the relationship you must maintain.

As servants of Christ, you and I are absolutely committed. We cannot call ourselves our own. We cannot call anything we have our own. Slaves in the ancient world had no rights at all. They were their masters' possession, whole and entire. So we must see ourselves in relation to Jesus, for that is how it is. We are his to do anything, to go anywhere, to undertake any task for him—and not to complain. Slaves have no right to complain.

"Shepherds after God's Own Heart," 14-15

REFLECT: As Christ's saved one, I am his slave, ready to do whatever he asks.

He called the crowd to him along with his disciples and said: "If anyone would come after me, he must deny himself and take up his cross and follow me."

Mark 8:34

Jesus Christ demands self-denial, that is, self-negation, as a necessary condition of discipleship. Self-denial is a summons to submit to the authority of God as Father and of Jesus as Lord and to declare lifelong war on one's instinctive egoism. What is to be negated is not personal self or one's existence as a rational and responsible human being. Jesus does not plan to turn us into zombies, nor does he ask us to volunteer for a robot role. The required denial is of carnal self, the egocentric, self-deifying urge with which we were born and which dominates us so ruinously in our natural state. Jesus represents discipleship as a matter of following him, and following him as based on taking up one's cross in self-negation.

Hot Tub Religion, 72-73

REFLECT: Following Jesus means giving up selfishness.

We know that in all things God works for the good of those who love him, who have been called according to his purpose. For those God foreknew he also predestined to be conformed to the likeness of his Son, that he might be the firstborn among many brothers.

Romans 8:28-29

All the experiences that make up the emotional reality of our lives—joys and sorrows, fulfillments and frustrations, delights and disappointments, happinesses and hurts—are part of God's curriculum for us in the school of holiness, to reshape us in the moral likeness of Jesus Christ.

It is reported that on one occasion when Teresa of Avila was traveling, her conveyance dumped her in the mud. The spunky saint's first words as she struggled to her feet were: "Lord, if this is how you treat your friends, it is no wonder that you have so few!" One of the most attractive things about Teresa is that she could be playful like this with her God. But none knew better than she that the ups and downs of her life were divinely planted in order to mold her character, enlarge her heart, and deepen her devotion. And what was true for her is true for us all.

Rediscovering Holiness, 16-17

REFLECT: Both ups and downs can make me more like Jesus.

We do not have a high priest who is unable to sympathize with our weaknesses, but we have one who has been tempted in every way, just as we are—yet was without sin. Let us then approach the throne of grace with confidence, so that we may receive mercy and find grace to help us in our time of need.

Hebrews 4:15-16

Jesus Christ, our risen Lord, is the same today as yesterday, and it belongs to the true Easter faith to take to our own hurts the healing of the Emmaus Road (see Luke 24:13-35). How? First, by telling Jesus our trouble, as he invites us to do each day. He remains a good listener, with what the hymn calls "a fellow-feeling for our pains"; and only as we lay aside prayerless resentment and self-pity and open our hearts to him will we know his help. Second, by letting him minister to us from Scripture, relating that which gives us pain to God's purpose of saving love: this will regularly mean looking to the Lord's human agents in ministry, as well as private Bible study. Third, by asking him to assure us that as we go through what feels like fire and floods he goes with us, and will stay with us till the road ends. This prayer he will always answer. The counsel from the Book of Hebrews was written long ago to ill-treated, distracted, and depressed believers. The Emmaus Road story urges us to do as it says—and it also shows us how.

"Walking to Emmaus with the Great Physician," 23

REFLECT: Jesus enters into my pain and will go through hardships with me.

Not everyone who says to me, "Lord, Lord," will enter the king-dom of heaven, but only he who does the will of my Father who is in heaven. Many will say to me on that day, "Lord, Lord, did we not prophesy in your name, and in your name drive out demons and perform many miracles?" Then I will tell them plainly, "I never knew you. Away from me, you evildoers!"

Matthew 7:21-23

The doctrine of preservation declares that the regenerate are saved through persevering in faith and Christian living to the end, and that it is God who keeps them persevering. This does not mean that all who ever professed conversion will be saved. False professions are made; short-term enthusiasts fall away. Only those who show themselves to be regenerate by pursuing heart-holiness and true neighbor-love as they pass through this world are entitled to believe themselves secure in Christ. Persevering in faith and penitence, not just in Christian formalism, is the path to glory. To suppose that believing in perseverance leads to careless living and arrogant presumption is a total misconception.

Concise Theology, 242

REFLECT: Once I am born again, I will continue following Christ to the end.

The fruit of the Spirit is love, joy, peace, patience, kindness, goodness, faithfulness, gentleness and self-control. Against such things there is no law.

Galatians 5:22-23

Love is the Christlike reaction to people's malice.

Joy is the Christlike reaction to depressing circumstances.

Peace is the Christlike reaction to troubles, threats, and invitations to anxiety.

Patience is the Christlike reaction to all that is maddening.

Kindness is the Christlike reaction to all who are unkind.

Goodness is the Christlike reaction to bad people and bad behavior.

Faithfulness and *gentleness* are the Christlike reactions to lies and fury.

Self-control is the Christlike reaction to every situation that goads you to lose your cool and hit out.

Rediscovering Holiness, 174

REFLECT: The Christlike reaction is never the expected response.

OCTOBER

God's will is not constant
comfort and worldly success.

Endure hardship as discipline.... No discipline seems pleasant at the time, but painful. Later on, however, it produces a harvest of righteousness and peace for those who have been trained by it.
Hebrews 12:7, 11

Eudaemonism is an uncommon word for which I should perhaps apologize. I use it because it is the only word I know that fits. It has nothing to do with demons. It comes from the Greek for "happy," *eudaimon,* and Webster defines it as "the system of philosophy which makes human happiness the highest object." I use the word as a label for the view that happiness means the presence of pleasure and freedom from all that is unpleasant. Eudaemonism says that since happiness is the supreme value, we may confidently look to God here and now to shield us from unpleasantness at every turn, or if unpleasantness breaks in, to deliver us from it immediately because it is never his will that we should have to live with it. This is a basic principle of much contemporary religion. Unhappily, however, it is also a false principle. It loses sight of the place of pain in sanctification whereby God trains his children to share his holiness. Such oversight can be ruinous.

Hot Tub Religion, 75

REFLECT: God's will is not that I should every moment feel happy, but that I should every moment be holy.

It has been granted to you on behalf of Christ not only to believe on him, but also to suffer for him.

Philippians 1:29

Christian endurance means living lovingly, joyfully, peacefully, and patiently under conditions that we wish were different. There is an umbrella word that we use to cover the countless situations that have this character: *suffering*. Suffering may be defined as getting what you do not want while wanting what you do not get.

Ours is not a good time for any sort of realism about suffering. We think of God as everyone's heavenly grandfather, there to lavish gifts upon us and enjoy us the way we are. We cherish shockingly strong illusions about having a right to expect from God health, wealth, ease, excitement, and sexual gratification. We are shockingly unaware that suffering Christianly is an integral aspect of biblical holiness, and a regular part of business as usual for the believer.

Rediscovering Holiness, 249-250

REFLECT: As a Christian believer, I can expect to suffer.

Our light and momentary troubles are achieving for us an eternal glory that far outweighs them all.

2 Corinthians 4:17

Suffering is the Christian's road home; no other road leads there. The twentieth-century West, however, has come to think of a life free from pain and trouble as virtually a natural human right, and Christian minds have been so swamped by this thinking that nowadays any pain and loss in a Christian's life is felt to cast doubt on God's goodness. It is perhaps no wonder that our age has produced the gospel of health and wealth, promising that God will give us right now whatever we name and claim under either heading. But if we can learn to take the Holy Spirit seriously once more, he will convince us afresh of the naturalness of suffering in the Christian life, probably by leading us into a higher degree of it than we have yet had to face.

"Introduction: On Being Serious
about the Holy Spirit," xv

REFLECT: Suffering is a natural and necessary part of the Christian life.

In fact, everyone who wants to live a godly life in Christ Jesus will be persecuted, while evil men and impostors will go from bad to worse, deceiving and being deceived.

2 Timothy 3:12-13

There are going to be casualties. People are going to let us down. There will be pain and grief. Are we budgeting realistically for that fact, or are we Pollyannas who suppose that if we are right with God it will be glory, glory all the way, and no troubles for anyone at all while we are around? It was not like that for Paul. It was not like that for Timothy. It will not be like that for us. To be sure, one who has prepared himself for trouble may find that in the goodness of God there are times when trouble does not come, and that brings joy and rejoicing. But those who are unprepared for difficulty and discouragement will find themselves terribly shaken when things do go wrong and get harder, as for all of us, sooner or later, they surely will.

"Shepherds after God's Own Heart," 16-17

REFLECT: Bad things do happen to God's people.

Now that same day two of them were going to a village called Emmaus.... As they talked... with each other, Jesus himself came up and walked along with them; but they were kept from recognizing him. He asked them, "What are you discussing together as you walk along?" They stood still, their faces downcast.

Luke 24:13-17

Here is a perfect instance of a kind of spiritual perplexity which every child of God experiences sooner or later. Be warned: it can be appallingly painful, and if you are not prepared to meet it, it can embitter you, maim you emotionally, and to a great extent destroy you—which, be it said, is Satan's goal in it, every time. What happens is that you find yourself feeling that God plays cat and mouse with you. Having lifted you up by giving you hope, he now throws you down by destroying it. What he gave you to lean on he suddenly takes away, and down you go. Your feelings say that he is playing games with you; that he must be a heartless, malicious ogre after all. So you feel broken in pieces, and no wonder. Do not say that these things never happen to truly faithful folk: you know perfectly well they do. And when they do, the pain is increased by the feeling that God has turned against you and is actively destroying the hopes that he himself once gave you.

"Walking to Emmaus with the Great Physician," 21

REFLECT: True faith does not immunize me against dashed hopes.

Be self-controlled and alert. Your enemy the devil prowls around like a roaring lion looking for someone to devour.

1 Peter 5:8

We are all prone to damaging delusions. There are delusions of theological error, of doubt and unbelief, of self-confidence; there are delusions that disrupt relationships. And then there are delusions about the Christian life—that it will ordinarily be easy, successful, healthy and wealthy, excitingly punctuated by miracles; that such acts as fornication and tax evasion will not matter as long as nobody finds out; that God always wants you to do what you feel like doing; and so on, and so on. Satan, the father of lies and a past master at deluding, labors constantly to mislead and muddle God's people, so that humble self-suspicion, and the commonsensical hard-headedness that used to be called prudence, and the habit of testing by Scripture things hitherto taken for granted, become virtues of very great importance.

Rediscovering Holiness, 42-43

REFLECT: It is a delusion to expect the Christian life to be easy.

A time is coming, and has come, when you will be scattered....
You will leave me all alone. I have told you these things, so that
in me you may have peace. In this world you will have trouble.
But take heart! I have overcome the world.

John 16:32-33

Growth in grace does not shield one from strains, pains, and pressures in one's Christian life. That growing Christians enjoy God's gift of peace is true, but the peace in question is relational:

- peace with God himself through the peacemaking blood of Christ;
- peace with circumstances, which, however harrowing, God has promised to order for our good (that is, our growth in grace);
- peace with themselves, for Christ's forgiving and accepting them requires them to forgive and accept themselves; and
- peace with those around them, to whom at Jesus' bidding they go as peacemakers.

Growing Christians grow in peace, but their growing in grace often has them groaning in grace as Christlike compassion comes more and more to possess their hearts. God does not mean the lives of his children in his tragically spoiled world to be sorrow-free, and we may confidently say that any who are sorrow-free are certainly not growing in grace.

Rediscovering Holiness, 186-187

REFLECT: God's grace does not shield me from sorrow.

God is faithful; he will not let you be tempted beyond what you can bear. But when you are tempted, he will also provide a way out so that you can stand up under it.

1 Corinthians 10:13

Suffering must be valued. Does that thought startle you? It should not. The world, of course, does not find value in suffering. It has no reason to. But Christians are in a different position, for the Bible assures us that God sanctifies our suffering to good ends. We are not to pretend, out of stoical pride, that we feel no pain or distress. Equally, however, we are not to spend all our time brooding on how we suffer, for that is sinful self-absorption. In any case, there are more important things to do. Our task is to take suffering in stride, not as if it is a pleasure (it isn't), but in the knowledge that God will not let it overwhelm us.

Rediscovering Holiness, 254-255

REFLECT: God promises that I will not be overcome by suffering.

Consider it pure joy, my brothers, whenever you face trials of many kinds, because you know that the testing of your faith develops perseverance. Perseverance must finish its work so that you may be mature and complete, not lacking anything.

James 1:2-4

When children are allowed to do what they like and are constantly shielded from situations in which their feelings might get hurt, we describe them as spoiled. When we say that, we are saying that overindulgent parenthood not only makes them unattractive today but also fails to prepare them for the moral demands of adult life tomorrow—two evils for the price of one. But God, who always has his eye on tomorrow as he deals with us today, never spoils his children, and the lifelong training course in holy living in which he enrolls us challenges and tests us to the utmost again and again. Christlike habits are ingrained most deeply as we learn to maintain them through experiences of pain and unpleasantness, which in retrospect appear as God's chisel for sculpting our souls.

Hot Tub Religion, 77

REFLECT: Pain is the chisel God uses to sculpt my soul.

I tell you the truth, unless a kernel of wheat falls to the ground and dies, it remains only a single seed. But if it dies, it produces many seeds.

John 12:24

Suffering fulfills the law of harvest. That law can be stated thus: before there is blessing anywhere, there will first be suffering somewhere. Scripture does not explain this, but simply sets it before us as a fact. Jesus requires all who are his to live by the same law of harvest that he lived by himself, becoming the seed that dies to bring forth fruit. Every experience of pain, grief, frustration, disappointment, and being hurt by others is a little death. When we serve the Savior in our worldly world, there are many such deaths to be died. But the call to us is to endure, since God sanctifies our endurance for fruitfulness in the lives of others.

Rediscovering Holiness, 262-263

REFLECT: Before blessing, suffering.

Praise be to the God and Father of our Lord Jesus Christ, the Father of compassion and the God of all comfort, who comforts us in all our troubles, so that we can comfort those in any trouble with the comfort we ourselves have received from God.
2 Corinthians 1:3-4

Through the pounding we experience we are, so to speak, broken up small so that each bit of what we are may become food for some hungry soul: food, that is, in the sense of empathetic insight and supportive wisdom. The hard and bitter experiences that now ravage you, like the death of a loved one (one example), are fitting you to be a channel of God's life to someone else. The true answer to the question, Why is this happening to me? will often be: It is not chastening or correction for yesterday's moral lapses. It has nothing to do with the past at all. It has to do only with the use God plans to make of you tomorrow, and how you need to be prepared for that. So you should expect hardship in some form to continue all your days.

Rediscovering Holiness, 263-264

REFLECT: My suffering can make me a channel of God's life.

Jesus called out with a loud voice, "Father, into your hands I commit my spirit." When he had said this, he breathed his last.

Luke 23:46

The way to deal with suffering in any form—from the mildest irritation to the mental and physical agony that so absorbs and overwhelms you that you groan and scream—is to offer it to the God who has permitted it, telling him to make what he wills of it, and of us through it. Contemplative prayer is often pictured as a loving look Godward, without at that moment either spoken words or active thoughts. It is contemplative prayer also when the Godward look is submissive, at a time when all power of thought and speech has been swamped by pain. Jesus on the cross is the model for this.

Rediscovering Holiness, 265-266

REFLECT: I can, like Jesus, offer my suffering to God.

Brothers, as an example of patience in the face of suffering, take the prophets who spoke in the name of the Lord. As you know, we consider blessed those who have persevered. You have heard of Job's perseverance and have seen what the Lord finally brought about. The Lord is full of compassion and mercy.

James 5:10-11

Job was never told about the challenge God met by allowing Satan to plague his servant. All Job knew was that the omnipotent God was morally perfect and that it would be blasphemously false to deny his goodness under any circumstances. He refused to "curse God" even when his livelihood, his children, and his health had been taken from him. Though not without struggle, Job held fast his integrity throughout the time of testing and maintained his confidence in God's goodness. And his confidence was vindicated. Did the bewildering series of catastrophes that overtook Job mean that God had abandoned his servant? Not at all. But the reason God had plunged him into darkness was never revealed to him. Now may not God, for wise purposes of his own, treat others of his followers as he treated Job?

Hot Tub Religion, 20-21

REFLECT: If I really have confidence in God, I will trust him even when I don't understand.

Those who suffer according to God's will should commit them-selves to their faithful Creator and continue to do good.

1 Peter 4:19

The heart of true religion is to glorify God by patient endurance and to praise him for his gracious deliverances. It is to live one's life, through smooth and rough places alike, in sustained obedience and thanksgiving for mercy received. It is to seek and find one's deepest joy, not in spiritual lotus-eating, but in discovering through each successive storm and conflict the mighty adequacy of Christ to save. It is the sure knowledge that God's way is best, both for our own welfare and for his glory. No problems of providence will shake the faith of the one who has truly learned this.

Hot Tub Religion, 26

REFLECT: When God wills me to suffer, I glorify him by patient endurance.

We do not want you to become lazy, but to imitate those who through faith and patience inherit what has been promised.

Hebrews 6:12

Patience means living out the belief that God orders everything for the spiritual good of his children. Patience does not just grin and bear things, stoic-like, but accepts them cheerfully as therapeutic workouts planned by a heavenly trainer who is resolved to get you up to full fitness. Patience, therefore, treats each situation as a new opportunity to honor God in a way that would otherwise not be possible, and acts accordingly. Patience breasts each wave of pressure as it rolls in, rejoicing to prove that God can keep one from losing his or her footing. And patience belongs to the ninefold fruit of the Spirit, which is the sanctifying profile Jesus set for his disciples.

"A Bad Trip," 12

REFLECT: Patience accepts trials as opportunities for growth.

Dear friend, I pray that you may enjoy good health and that all may go well with you, even as your soul is getting along well.

3 John 2

John's words alert us to the twin truths that personal health is more than physical well-being, and that health of soul (mind and heart) is ultimately more important than the well-being of the body. That is something we must never forget. Sometimes God sends us people whose physical condition effectively reminds us that this is so. Joni Eareckson Tada, a quadriplegic with a marvelous ministry who spends her days in a wheelchair, is one such. Twice it has been my privilege to introduce Joni from a platform. Each time I have ventured to predict that her message would show her to be the healthiest person in the building—a prediction which, so far as I could judge, came true both times. The secret of total health is to accept one's lack of physical well-being as from God, to offer it back to him to make what he can of it for his own praise, and to ask him to keep you sweet, steady, and patient as you live with it.

Rediscovering Holiness, 158-159

REFLECT: As one can be a sick person with a body that works well, so one can be a healthy person with a body that is a wreck, even a mass of pain.

We are hard pressed on every side, but not crushed; perplexed, but not in despair; persecuted, but not abandoned; struck down, but not destroyed. We always carry around in our body the death of Jesus, so that the life of Jesus may also be revealed in our body.

2 Corinthians 4:8-10

In a self-centered, pleasure-oriented, self-indulgent world like ours today, this sounds most brutal and chilling. But it is, in fact, the true meaning of the time-honored dictum, "Man's extremity is God's opportunity." Opportunity for what?—to show his power, the power of his grace, now displayed for the praise of his glory. Being weak and feeling weak is not in itself fun. One might have expected God to use his power to eliminate weakness from the lives of his servants. In fact, however, what he does again and again is to make his weak servants into wonders of wisdom, love, and helpfulness to others despite their disability. It is thus that he loves to show his power.

Rediscovering Holiness, 233

REFLECT: God's power becomes visible through human weakness.

The Lord stood at my side and gave me strength.

2 Timothy 4:17

The Lord first makes us conscious of our weakness, so that our heart cries out, "I can't handle this." We go to the Lord to ask him to remove the burden that we feel is crushing us. But Christ replies, "In my strength you *can* handle this, and in answer to your prayer, I will *strengthen* you to handle it." Thus in the end our testimony, like Paul's, is: "I can do everything through him who *gives me strength*" (Philippians 4:13). We find ourselves living (if I may put it this way) baptismally, with resurrection-out-of-death as the recurring shape of our experience. And we realize with ever-growing clarity that this is the fullest and profoundest expression of the empowered Christian life.

Rediscovering Holiness, 236-237

REFLECT: My weakness is an opportunity for Christ's strength.

God chose the weak things of the world to shame the wise.
1 Corinthians 1:27

If I could remember, each day of my life, that the way to grow stronger is to grow weaker, if I would accept that each day's frustrations, obstacles, and accidents are God's ways of making me acknowledge my weakness, so that growing stronger might become a possibility for me, if I did not betray myself into relying on myself—my knowledge, my expertise, my position, my skill with words, and so on—so much of the time, what a difference it would make to me! I wonder how many others, besides myself, need to concentrate on learning these lessons? May God in his great mercy weaken us all!

Rediscovering Holiness, 238

REFLECT: The way to grow stronger is to grow weaker.

We who are alive are always being given over to death for Jesus'
sake, so that his life may be revealed in our mortal body.
2 Corinthians 4:11

Why does God shape his children's lives in a way that
keeps them feeling weak and swamped? Why do believers
constantly find thorns in their flesh and in their beds? Why
does the God of sovereign love periodically plunge his
beloved ones into suffering and strain? Paul's testimony tells
us partly why. "We were under great pressure, far beyond our
ability to endure, so that we despaired even of life.... But this
happened that we might not rely on ourselves but on God"
(2 Corinthians 1:8-9). "For Christ's sake, I delight in weaknesses, in insults, in hardships, in persecutions, in difficulties.
For when I am weak, then I am strong" (2 Corinthians
12:10). Exactly! What the world never understands—and
what those who think that the good Christian feels strong
and powerful and has life easy never understand—is that only
consciously weak souls ever lean hard enough on the Lord to
stand steady or walk straight in his risen power.

"The Way of the Weak Is the Only Healthy Way," 28

REFLECT: Weakness is the true Christian path, the only
healthy way.

By the grace given me I say to every one of you: Do not think of yourself more highly than you ought, but rather think of yourself with sober judgment, in accordance with the measure of faith God has given you.

Romans 12:3

We grow *up* into Christ by growing *down* into lowliness (humility, from the Latin word *humilis,* meaning low). Christians, we might say, grow greater by getting smaller.

Of his own ministry, in relation to that of the Lord Jesus, John the Baptist declared: "He must become greater; I must become less" (John 3:30). Of our lives as believers, something similar has to be said. Pride blows us up like balloons, but grace punctures our conceit and lets the hot, proud air out of our system. The result is that we shrink, and end up seeing ourselves as less—less nice, less able, less wise, less good, less strong, less steady, less committed, less of a piece— than ever we thought we were. We stop kidding ourselves that we are persons of great importance to the world and to God. We settle for being insignificant and dispensable.

Rediscovering Holiness, 120

REFLECT: As a Christian, I grow greater by growing smaller.

My heart is not proud, O LORD,
my eyes are not haughty;
I do not concern myself with great matters
or things too wonderful for me.
But I have stilled and quieted my soul;
like a weaned child with its mother,
like a weaned child is my soul within me.

Psalm 131:1-2

It is impossible at the same time to give the impression both that I am a great Christian and that Jesus Christ is a great Master. So the Christian will practice curling up small, as it were, so that in and through him or her the Savior may show himself great.

Offloading our fantasies of omnicompetence, we start trying to be trustful, obedient, dependent, patient, and willing in our relationship to God. We give up our dreams of being greatly admired for doing wonderfully well. We begin teaching ourselves unemotionally and matter-of-factly to recognize that we are not likely ever to appear, or actually to be, much of a success by the world's standards. We bow to events that rub our noses in the reality of our own weaknesses, and we look to God for strength quietly to cope. That is what I mean by growing downward.

Rediscovering Holiness, 121

REFLECT: I must give up my craving for success and learn to live by God's strength.

My son, do not make light of the Lord's discipline, and do not lose heart when he rebukes you, because the Lord disciplines those he loves, and he punishes everyone he accepts as a son.

Hebrews 12:5-6

It is extraordinary how little the New Testament says about God's interest in our success, by comparison with the enormous amount it says about God's interest in our holiness, our maturity in Christ, and our growth into the fullness of his image. Typical of his revealed interest is his message through the writer of Hebrews to a group of converts who were being harassed because of their Christian faith. God does not promise to shield them from trouble. Instead, he tells them that they must be ready to shed their blood rather than yield to pressure and renounce their faith. Moreover, they must understand that hardship is the discipline by means of which their heavenly Father hammers them into shape for a harvest of holiness. If they were not being thus hammered, they would have reason to doubt whether they were his children at all. Strong stuff!—but it makes crystal clear what we need to know: God's priority in all his dealings with us is to make us holy.

Rediscovering Holiness, 215

REFLECT: God asks me to be holy, not successful.

Make the heart of this people calloused;
make their ears dull
and close their eyes.
Otherwise they might see with their eyes,
hear with their ears,
understand with their hearts,
and turn and be healed.

Isaiah 6:10

God was warning Isaiah that his message was going to be rejected, so that the effect of his ministry would be to leave people less sensitive to spiritual things than before (for hearts are always calloused by saying no to God). In the same way, we who speak for Christ today must be prepared to find that what we say is disregarded and we are laboring with little or no visible success. Like Isaiah, we are called to be faithful, not necessarily fruitful. Faithfulness is our business; fruitfulness is an issue that we must be content to leave with God. Visible success in the form of instant results is not guaranteed in Christian ministry.

Hot Tub Religion, 56

REFLECT: God asks me to be faithful, not successful.

The Pharisees, who loved money, heard all this and were sneering at Jesus. He said to them, "You are the ones who justify yourselves in the eyes of men, but God knows your hearts. What is highly valued among men is detestable in God's sight."

Luke 16:14-15

On my desk as I write lies a broadsheet for pastors that begins with the banner headline, "How Will I Know When I've Succeeded?" The burden of the broadsheet is that pastors must be proactive rather than reactive, committed to mission and outreach rather than maintenance and marking time, and that for this they need a philosophy of ministry—that is, a thought-out rationale of ends and means. Defined goals, it says, give you direction, generate energy, sustain morale (because now you know where you are going), show you what on a daily basis is important for you and so deliver you from the tyranny of the merely urgent, facilitate team building and the eliciting of cooperation and support, and enable you to evaluate how you are doing; and all of that is true and valuable. But we can succeed in reaching our goals and still not know God's verdict on what we have been up to. The fact that I have thus succeeded does not mean that God now necessarily counts me a success.

A Passion for Faithfulness, 206-207

REFLECT: Human success may be worthless in God's sight.

After Uzziah became powerful, his pride led to his downfall. He was unfaithful to the LORD his God.

2 Chronicles 26:16

Where success is god, pride always grows strong and spreads through the soul. The fruit of nourished pride is invariably bitter. Orienting all Christian action to visible success as its goal, a move which to many moderns seems supremely sensible and businesslike, is a seedbed both of unspiritual vainglory for the self-rated succeeders and of unspiritual despair for the self-rated failures, and a source of shallowness and superficiality all round. After setting biblically appropriate goals, embracing biblically appropriate means of seeking to realize them, assessing as best we can where we have got to in pursuing them, and making any course corrections that our assessments suggest, the way of health and humility is for us to admit to ourselves that in the final analysis we do not and cannot know the measure of our success as God sees fit. Wisdom says: leave success ratings to God, and live your Christianity as a religion of faithfulness rather than an idolatry of achievement.

A Passion for Faithfulness, 208-209

REFLECT: A success mentality leads to pride and despair.

When pride comes, then comes disgrace,
but with humility comes wisdom.

Proverbs 11:2

Sobriety about one's powers is a character trait that betokens real humility and maturity before God. Being humble is not a matter of pretending to be worthless, but is a form of realism, not only regarding the real badness of one's sins and stupidities and the real depth of one's dependence on God's grace, but also regarding the real range of one's abilities. Humble believers know what they can and cannot do. They note both their gifts and their limitations, and so are able to avoid both the unfaithfulness of letting their God-given powers lie fallow and the foolhardiness of biting off more than they can chew.

A Passion for Faithfulness, 48

REFLECT: Humility is realism.

He guides the humble in what is right and teaches them his way.
Psalm 25:9

The radios of my youth would crackle with atmospherics, making clear reception impossible. All forms of self-centeredness and self-indulgence, from surface-level indiscipline and lawlessness to the subtlety of grandiose elitism or the irreverence of not obeying the guidance we have received already, will act as atmospherics in the heart, making recognition of God's will harder than it should be, and our testing of impressions less thorough and exact. But those who are being led by the Spirit into humble holiness will also be led by the Spirit in judging their impressions, and so will increasingly be enabled to distinguish the Spirit's own nudges from the posturings of impure and improper desire. He teaches the *humble* his way. Blessed, then, we may say, are the pure in heart, for they shall know the will of God.

"True Guidance," 39

REFLECT: Humility and wisdom walk hand in hand.

They were all trying to frighten us, thinking, "Their hands will get too weak for the work, and it will not be completed." But I prayed, "Now strengthen my hands."

Nehemiah 6:9

William Temple said somewhere that whereas we think our real work is our activity, to which prayer is an adjunct, our praying is our real work, and our activity is the index of how we have done it. Surely Temple is right. For real prayer—prayer, that is, that centers on the hallowing of God's name and the doing of his will—purifies the heart, purges our attitudes and motives, melts down all the self-centeredness, self-sufficiency, and self-reliance that as fallen creatures we bring to it, and programs us to work humbly, in a God-honoring, God-fearing, God-dependent way. We need to remember that in God's sight motivation is an integral element in action, and any motivation that exalts self will render our work rotten at the core. Because of the self-absorbed habits of our sinful hearts, the only way to anything like pure motives is to pray persistently about the things we do and ask ourselves constantly before the Lord why we are doing them and how they fit in with God's glory and the good of his people.

A Passion for Faithfulness, 79-80

REFLECT: Prayer programs me to work humbly, depending on God.

Christ Jesus came into the world to save sinners—of whom I am the worst. But for that very reason I was shown mercy so that in me, the worst of sinners, Christ Jesus might display his unlimited patience as an example for those who would believe on him and receive eternal life.

1 Timothy 1:15-16

Those who are growing in grace increase in the spirit of doxology and worship. They are less and less self-absorbed and self-concerned. There is a kind of balance effect that operates here. If your pride and conceit are rising, your concern about praising God will be diminishing. But if your passion for praise is growing, then your sense of your own dignity will decline. You will be following in the footsteps of Paul who, writing to the Corinthians about AD 57 or 58, spoke of himself as the "least of the apostles"; who, writing to the Ephesians about AD 61 or 62, spoke of himself as "less than the least of all God's people"; and who, writing to Timothy about AD 65 or 66, spoke of himself as the "worst of sinners." These phrases show that his estimate of himself was going down. As a result, he increasingly breaks out into doxology, which shows how passionately his heart longed to exalt and praise God.

"The Means of Growth," 8-9

REFLECT: There is no growth in grace without increase in the spirit of humble praise.

There is a time for everything,
and a season for every activity under heaven: ...
a time to weep and a time to laugh,
a time to mourn and a time to dance.

Ecclesiastes 3:1, 4

A moment of conscious triumph makes one feel that after this nothing will really matter; a moment of realized disaster makes one feel that this is the end of everything. But neither feeling is realistic, for neither event is really what it is felt to be. The circumstances of triumph will not last, and the moment of triumph will sooner or later give way to moments of disappointment, strain, frustration, and grief, while the circumstances of disaster will prove to have in them seeds of recovery and new hope. Life in this world under God's providence is like that; it always has been and always will be; it is so in the Bible, and it remains so as the twentieth century gives way to the twenty-first. The mature person, who is mentally and emotionally an adult as distinct from a child, knows this and does not forget it.

A Passion for Faithfulness, 200

REFLECT: In this world, neither triumph nor disaster is permanent.

NOVEMBER

God wills us to grow
in grace and joy.

Peter, an apostle of Jesus Christ, to God's elect,... who have been chosen according to the foreknowledge of God the Father, through the sanctifying work of the Spirit, for obedience to Jesus Christ and sprinkling by his blood: Grace and peace be yours in abundance.

1 Peter 1:1-2

Sound spirituality needs to be thoroughly Trinitarian. Neglect the *Son,* lose your focus on his mediation and blood atonement and heavenly intercession, and you slip back into the legalism that is fallen man's natural religion, the treadmill religion of works. Again, neglect the *Spirit,* lose your focus on the fellowship with Christ that he creates, the renewing of nature that he effects, the assurance and joy that he evokes, and the enabling for service that he bestows, and you slip back into orthodoxism and formalism, the religion of aspiration and perspiration without either inspiration or transformation, the religion of low expectations, deep ruts, and grooves that become graves. Finally, neglect the *Father,* lose your focus on the tasks he prescribes and the discipline he inflicts, and you become a mushy, soft-centered, self-indulgent, unsteady, lazy, spoiled child in the divine family, making very heavy weather of any troubles and setbacks that come.

"An Introduction to Systematic Spirituality," 7

REFLECT: The Trinity is the source of the Christian's spiritual growth.

The Counselor, the Holy Spirit, whom the Father will send in my name, will teach you all things and will remind you of everything I have said to you.

John 14:26

The Holy Spirit is not an impersonal force put at our disposal or harnessed to our wills; rather, the Spirit is a sovereign person who at his own will, which is also the will of the Father and the Son, disposes of us. The Spirit operates in and through our thinking, our decision making, and our affections.

His blessing on the Bible we read, and on the Christian instruction we receive, persuades us of the truth of Christianity. He shows us how God's promises and demands bear on our lives. His new-creative action at the center of our personal being so changes and energizes us that we do in fact obey the truth. The persuasion at the conscious level is powerful. The heart-changing action that produces Christian commitment is almighty. First to last, however, the power exercised is personal.

Rediscovering Holiness, 226

REFLECT: The Holy Spirit is a living person, not a mere force.

If you are led by the Spirit, you are not under law.
Galatians 5:18

What does it mean to be "led by the Spirit"? The Spirit leads, first, by giving us understanding of the biblical guidelines within which we must keep, the biblical goals at which we must aim, and the biblical models that we should imitate, plus the bad examples from which we are meant to take warning. He leads, second, by giving us wisdom through prayerful thought and taking advice to see how we can best follow this biblical teaching. He leads, third, by making us want God's glory and growth in grace, with the result that our vision of spiritual priorities becomes constantly clearer, and our resources of wisdom and experience for making each next decision when the time comes are constantly increased. He leads, finally, by making us delight in God's will as we discern it, so that we find ourselves wanting to do it because we know that it is the good way for us to walk in.

"True Guidance," 36

REFLECT: The Spirit leads me by transforming my whole life.

Woe to those who... say, "Let God hurry,
let him hasten his work
so we may see it.
Let it approach,
let the plan of the Holy One of Israel come,
so we may know it."

Isaiah 5:18-19

In God's hospital, the course of treatment that the Father, Son, and Holy Spirit, the permanent medical staff (if I dare so to speak), are administering to us is called *sanctification*, which has as its goal our final restoration to the fullness of the divine image. It is a process that includes, on the one hand, medication and diet (in the form of biblical instruction and admonition coming in various ways to the heart) and, on the other hand, tests and exercises (in the form of internal and external pressures, providentially ordered, to which we have to make active response). The process goes on as long as we are in this world, which is something that God determines in each case. Like patients in any hospital, we are impatient for recovery. But God knows what he is doing; sometimes, for reasons connected with the maturity and ministry that he has in view for us, he makes haste slowly. That is something we have to learn humbly to accept. We are in a hurry; he is not.

"The Reality Cure," 35

REFLECT: Sanctification takes a lifetime.

Each one should test his own actions. Then he can take pride in himself, without comparing himself to somebody else.

Galatians 6:4

Those who compare themselves with each other, says Paul, are not wise. One reason why this is so is that God does not deal with us all at just the same points, at just the same time, or at just the same pace. If we want to measure ourselves, let us rather ask: What am I able to do because I am a Christian living in the faith and strength of Christ today that I was never able to do before I was a Christian? It is no great thing if a person who was nice before he was converted remains nice afterward. But it is a triumph of grace when a person like Peter, who was unstable as water before Pentecost, is suddenly turned into a strong, steady man. What do you find yourself able to do through Christ today which you were never able to do before? If you have an answer to that question, you have a testimony to a real measure of growth in grace.

"The Means of Growth," 7

REFLECT: God's grace changes me.

Let us stop passing judgment on one another. Instead, make up your mind not to put any stumbling block or obstacle in your brother's way.

Romans 14:13

The precise quality of change involved in people's growth in grace is always conditioned by their natural make-up. It is easy to underestimate the Holy Spirit's achievement in the lives of those who suffer from badly flawed temperaments or characters. The only generalizations it is safe to make are these:

- moral and spiritual Christlikeness is the goal in every case;
- all Christians can testify that knowing God through Jesus Christ enables them now to live and act in ways that were simply beyond them before; and
- a professed Christian with no such testimony can hardly be genuine and is certainly not growing in grace.

Rediscovering Holiness, 183-185

REFLECT: Growth in grace is affected by my nature.

We pray this in order that you may live a life worthy of the Lord and may please him in every way: bearing fruit in every good work, growing in the knowledge of God.

Colossians 1:10

It is a mistake to suppose that growth in grace is automatic, something you need not bother about because it will look after itself, something which is guaranteed, particularly if you are a professional minister, missionary, or church officer. The enemy wants to encourage all who seek to serve God to take it for granted that as we do our job we shall automatically grow and mature in Christ and therefore need not bother about sanctification at all. He wants to encourage us to think this way because, if we are not striving to grow, we are actually in danger of doing the very opposite, namely, shrinking as persons behind the role we play. Those of us who are clergy, I think, have over the years erred greatly here. We have concentrated on our role, and as individuals we have so often shrunk. We must not assume that growth will look after itself and proceed automatically if it is not our conscious concern.

"The Means of Growth," 8

REFLECT: Christian growth is not automatic.

If we claim to be without sin, we deceive ourselves and the truth is not in us.

1 John 1:8

Growth in grace is always growth by grace and under grace, never beyond grace. And grace means God enriching sinners. That is who we are. We never get to a point where we can cease to thank God for Calvary on a day-to-day basis and humble ourselves before him as hell-deserving sinners. There is no sinless perfection in this life. Sinless perfection is part of the hope of glory. Here, the best the Lord enables us to do is less than perfect, and we must constantly ask God to forgive what is defective. We shall never cease to be in this life hell-deserving sinners living daily by pardon. And God forbid that we should ever be found thinking in any other terms!

"The Means of Growth," 10-11

REFLECT: I need God's grace every day of my life.

If you think you are standing firm, be careful that you don't fall!

1 Corinthians 10:12

We are all invalids in God's hospital. In moral and spiritual terms we are all sick and damaged, diseased and deformed, scarred and sore, lame and lopsided, to a far, far greater extent than we realize. Christians today may imagine themselves to be strong, healthy, and holy when, in fact, they are actually weak, sick, and sinful in ways that are noticeable not just to their heavenly Father, but also to their fellow believers. Pride and complacency, however, blind us to this reality. We need to realize that the spiritual health we testify to is only partial and relative, a matter of being less sick and less incapacitated now than we were before. Measured by the absolute standard of spiritual health that we see in Jesus Christ, we are all of us no more, just as we are no less, than invalids in process of being cured.

Rediscovering Holiness, 40-41

REFLECT: Under God's care I am getting better, but I am not yet well.

Why are you downcast, O my soul?
Why so disturbed within me?
Put your hope in God, for I will yet praise him,
my Savior and my God.

Psalm 42:5

God brings on dryness, with resultant restlessness of heart, in order to induce a new depth of humble, hopeful openness to himself, which he then crowns with a liberating and animating reassurance of his love—one that goes beyond anything that was sensed before. As Christ's humiliation and grief on the cross preceded his exaltation to the joy of his throne, so over and over again humbling experiences of impotence and frustration precede inward renewing, with a sense of triumph and glory, in the believer's heart. Thus, with wisdom adapted to each Christian's temperament, circumstances, and needs, our heavenly Father draws and binds his children closer to himself.

Rediscovering Holiness, 100-101

REFLECT: Times of dryness precede times of renewal.

I have learned to be content whatever the circumstances. I know what it is to be in need, and I know what it is to have plenty. I have learned the secret of being content in any and every situation, whether well fed or hungry, whether living in plenty or in want.

Philippians 4:11-12

It is a mistake to imagine that God's goal is our unbroken ease and comfort. It is, rather, our sanctification and Christlikeness, the true holiness that is the highway to happiness. Constant ease and comfort, therefore, are not to be expected. Yet Christians may nonetheless derive constant contentment from their knowledge that God is making everything that happens to them a means of furthering and realizing the glorious destiny that is theirs. "Whatever is good for God's children, they shall have it," wrote Richard Sibbes, the Puritan, "for all is theirs to further them to heaven. If crosses be good, they shall have them; if disgrace be good, they shall have it; for all is ours, to serve our main good." To understand this is to have the secret of abiding contentment in one's grasp.

Hot Tub Religion, 158

REFLECT: I will not have constant comfort, but I can learn constant contentment.

Everyone who competes in the games goes into strict training. They do it to get a crown that will not last; but we do it to get a crown that will last forever.

1 Corinthians 9:25

The call of God to develop fellowship with him, in the face of pressures and restraints imposed on us by our condition, our company, and our circumstances, along with our weaknesses and blind spots and the multitude of traps set for us by the devil, make imperative a planned, orderly, thoughtful approach to the business of daily living. Only then can we ever ensure that there is room in our lives for all the things we ought to be doing. As the children of this world, fired by personal ambition, set themselves career goals and then work very hard to achieve them, so God's children, fired by the greatness of divine love, should have before their minds the goal of discipline in daily living, and work equally hard, planning, praying, and trying things out, to make it a reality. The alternative is to live like a pilot flying blind—always being taken by surprise and tyrannized by the immediate, the urgent, and the unexpected—experiencing life as a succession of emergencies that one is never ready to meet.

Rediscovering Holiness, 116

REFLECT: Effective living for Christ requires planning and discipline.

They said to him, "May we know what this new teaching is that you are presenting? You are bringing some strange ideas to our ears, and we want to know what they mean." (All the Athenians and the foreigners who lived there spent their time doing nothing but talking about and listening to the latest ideas.)

Acts 17:19-21

In England at the turn of the century, Anglican evangelicals used to ask whether people had become *serious.* The question did not mean, have these folk become somber and long-faced? What was in question was whether these folk had begun to reckon seriously with God, Christ, the Bible, the gospel, their own sinfulness and guilt, and the issues of eternity, which are settled for good or ill by the choices we make now. In a narcissistic age like ours, the question of seriousness presses Christians uncomfortably. We can be bright believers, burbling away about our wonderful conversion, and still be living frivolous, unstable, ego-tripping lives. We run from one brief enthusiasm to another, constantly pursuing way-out novelties of belief and behavior, and earning for ourselves at home, in church, and in the wider community David Niven's biting comment on Errol Flynn: "At least you knew where you were with him; he always let you down." Steady seriousness is one mark of right-living Christians. Am I serious? Are you?

"Christian Gravitas in a Narcissistic Age," 46

REFLECT: It is better to hold a steady course than to pursue excitement.

I am sending you to them to open their eyes and turn them from darkness to light, and from the power of Satan to God, so that they may receive forgiveness of sins and a place among those who are sanctified by faith in me.

Acts 26:17-18

Conversion means commitment to God in response to mercy from God and consists of repentance and faith. In Scripture these two overlap. *Repentance* is not just regretful remorse but a total about-turn in one's thoughts, aims, and acts, so that one leaves the paths of self-willed disobedience to serve God in faith and faithfulness. *Faith* is not just believing Christian truth but forsaking self-confidence and manmade hopes to trust wholly in Christ and his cross for pardon, peace, and life, so that henceforth one lives to one's lover-God in thankful, penitent obedience. Conversion need not be dramatically sudden or emotional, nor does one have to be fully aware of what is happening (though a conscious conversion usually proves a blessing). What is crucial, however, is that the marks of conversion—faith and repentance as principles of daily living—should be found in us; otherwise, we cannot be judged Christians at all, whatever experiences we may claim. Thus, the converted lifestyle is more significant than any conversion experience.

Growing in Christ, 108

REFLECT: The converted life is based on repentance and faith.

Dear friends, since you already know this, be on your guard so that you may not be carried away by the error of lawless men and fall from your secure position. But grow in the grace and knowledge of our Lord and Savior Jesus Christ. To him be glory both now and forever! Amen.

2 Peter 3:17-18

Conversion must be continuous. For many Christians there is a moment of conscious conversion, and this experience is a great blessing. There has to be for all of us some form of entry into the converted state, in which none of us is found by nature. It is a happy thing to be able to recall how one's own entry into that state took place. But there is more: following on from "the hour I first believed," conversion must now become a lifelong process. It has been defined from this standpoint as a matter of giving as much as you know of yourself to as much as you know of God. This means that as our knowledge of God and ourselves grows (and the two grow together), so our conversion needs to be repeated and extended constantly.

Rediscovering Holiness, 139-140

REFLECT: Conversion is a lifelong process.

Brothers, if someone is caught in a sin, you who are spiritual should restore him gently. But watch yourself, or you also may be tempted.

Galatians 6:1

Let it be said that in declaring the eternal security of God's people it is clearer to speak of their preservation than, as is commonly done, of their perseverance. Perseverance means persistence under discouragement and contrary pressure. The assertion that believers persevere in faith and obedience despite everything is true, but the reason is that Jesus Christ through the Spirit persists in preserving them.

Sometimes the regenerate backslide and fall into gross sin. But in this they act out of character, do violence to their own new nature, and make themselves deeply miserable, so that eventually they seek and find restoration to righteousness. In retrospect, their lapse seems to them to have been madness. When regenerate believers act in character, they manifest a humble, grateful desire to please the God who saved them; and the knowledge that he is pledged to keep them safe forever simply increases this desire.

Concise Theology, 241-243

REFLECT: God preserves me from falling back into a life of sin.

Whatever is true, whatever is noble, whatever is right, whatever is pure, whatever is lovely, whatever is admirable—if anything is excellent or praiseworthy—think about such things.

Philippians 4:8

Can we really choose what we are going to think about? The idea of regularly choosing themes for our thoughts seems strange, but Paul has no doubt that it is possible. He actually commands it. Controlling and directing one's thoughts is a habit, and the more one practices it, the better one becomes at it. Motivation, of course, helps, and Christians have a deep-rooted urge, instinctive to them as regenerate persons, to center their thoughts on God's grace and glory at all times. It has always been common for Christians to let their thoughts be drawn up to God and to meditate—that is, talk to themselves and to God, silently or aloud, concerning God's nature, works, and ways, in a manner that prompts praise and adoration and brings endless delight to the heart. Paul's instruction in what to think about simply gives focus and direction to this regenerate instinct, so as to ensure that our meditation will profit us as much as possible.

Hot Tub Religion, 166-167

REFLECT: I can choose to focus my thoughts on God's good gifts.

May the God of hope fill you with all joy and peace as you trust in him, so that you may overflow with hope by the power of the Holy Spirit.

Romans 15:13

What, in particular, are the true, honorable, just, pure, lovely, gracious, excellent, and praiseworthy things on which we are to center our thoughts (see Philippians 4:8)? They are the doings of God and the fruit of those doings in human lives. They include the fourfold awareness that

1. God loves me, infinitely and eternally;
2. everything comes to me from God, at least with his permission and always under his protection, to further my eternal good;
3. my saving knowledge of the Lord Jesus, which will eternally increase, is something supremely worth having; and
4. the gospel message of salvation that I seek to pass on to others is something supremely worth giving.

These thoughts will always prime the pump of joy in our hearts and thus produce a steady flow of joy, peace, and delight. Try it and see!

Hot Tub Religion, 167

REFLECT: When I focus on God's work in my life, I experience joy and peace.

Her ways are pleasant ways, and all her paths are peace.

Proverbs 3:17

It is promised that wisdom's paths will be "pleasant ways," and that means, among other things, that if at first we find ourselves disliking what we see to be God's will for us, God will change us at that point if we let him. God is no sadist, directing us to do what we do not want to do so that he can see us suffer. Rather, he has joy in store for us in every course of action to which he leads us, even those from which we shrink at first and which do in fact involve outward unpleasantness.

"True Guidance," 36

REFLECT: God wants to change me so that I delight to do his will.

That which was from the beginning, which we have heard, which we have seen with our eyes, which we have looked at and our hands have touched—this we proclaim concerning the Word of life. We write this to make our joy complete.

1 John 1:1, 4

The secret of joy for believers lies in the fine art of Christian thinking. It is by this means that the Holy Spirit, over and above his special occasional visitations in moments of joy, regularly sustains in us the joy that marks us out as Christ's. Our Lord Jesus wants our joy to be full. Certainly, he has made abundant provision for our joy. And if we focus our minds on the facts from which joy flows, springs of joy will well up in our hearts every day of our lives, turning our ongoing pilgrimage through this world into an experience of contentment and exaltation of which the world knows nothing. From this experience of joy will come strength for service. Joy—that is, rejoicing in the Lord—is thus a basic discipline of the Christian life, essential to spiritual health and vitality. Few Christians seem to understand this, and fewer still seem to practice the discipline with diligence. But what a difference it makes when we do!

Hot Tub Religion, 168

REFLECT: Joy is an essential Christian discipline.

When God gives any man wealth and possessions, and enables him to enjoy them, to accept his lot and be happy in his work—this is a gift of God.

Ecclesiastes 5:19

Where does joy come from? If we consulted a professional counselor, we could expect to be told that joy springs from four sources.

First, joy flows from awareness of being loved. No one has joy who does not know that there is someone who values, accepts, and cares for him or her.

Second, joy flows from accepting one's situation as good. People who are always fretting about the way things are, wishing they were different, and longing for things to happen that are not likely to happen disqualify themselves from joy.

Third, joy flows from having something worthwhile. We speak of our spouses, our children, our homes, our books, our hobbies as our joys. What we mean is that in these relationships and activities we have something precious that makes life worth living.

Fourth, joy flows from giving something worth giving. Many go through life without ever learning that joy is like jam, sticking to you as you spread it, but that is the truth all the same.

Hot Tub Religion, 153-155

REFLECT: Joy is a result of my attitude, not my circumstances.

My brothers, rejoice in the Lord!

Philippians 3:1

The first source of joy is the awareness that one is loved. Christians know themselves loved in a way that no one else does, for they know that God the Father so loved them as to give his only Son to die on the cross in shame and agony so that they might have eternal life.

The second source of joy is the acceptance of one's situation as good. Christians can do this everywhere and always because they know that circumstances and experiences, pleasant and unpleasant alike, are planned out for them by their loving heavenly Father as part of their preparation for glory.

Joy's third source is possession of something worth possessing. Christians can, with Paul, celebrate the incomparable worth of the saving relationship with Christ that they now possess—or rather, that now possesses them.

The fourth source of joy is to give something worth giving. When Christians share their knowledge of Christ with others, they know they are giving them the one thing that is supremely worth giving and is, in addition, desperately needed.

Hot Tub Religion, 156-162

REFLECT: Christians have more reasons for joy than anyone else.

As the Father has loved me, so have I loved you. Now remain in my love. If you obey my commands, you will remain in my love, just as I have obeyed my Father's commands and remain in his love.

John 15:9-10

Our obligation to honor and obey God is binding just because we owe our very existence to him; yet it is vastly increased by his having so loved the world that he gave his Son to die so that whoever will might live, and by his having actually saved from sin and death us who believe. In both Testaments God's relation to his people is more than that of a great king to his subjects; it is also that of a father to his children; his royal covenant is a family covenant too, and his steadfast love is the faithful affection of a heavenly parent. Love ennobles the beloved, and response to God's authoritative claim by one who knows how God loves him will be felt as privilege, dignity, and delight. Thus life under God's authority comes to be experienced not as a demeaning misery, but as an enriching joy, and the more complete and self-abandoning our submission, the deeper our joy will be.

"The Reconstitution of Authority," 5-6

REFLECT: Joy comes from submission to God's authority.

This is love: that we walk in obedience to his commands. As you have heard from the beginning, his command is that you walk in love.

2 John 6

Christians know that before they came to Christ the anti-God allergy called "sin" ruled them, so that it was not in them to love God and neighbor. But they know too that grace aims to restore nature to righteousness, and that the Holy Spirit has made new creatures of them in Christ; for by uniting them to him in death and resurrection he has dethroned sin and implanted Christ's own instinct to love and worship the Father in holy obedience. They know that the indwelling Spirit now impels and enables them to practice godliness as never before, and that only as they live out what is literally the life of Christ in them will they find fulfillment and joy.

"How Christians Should Understand Themselves," 36

REFLECT: Joy is the fruit of holy obedience.

He who goes out weeping,
carrying seed to sow,
will return with songs of joy,
carrying sheaves with him.

Psalm 126:6

To readers enmeshed in the four down *Ds*—disappointment, desolation, depression, desperation—or bogged down in any one of the four forlorn *Fs*—frustration, failure, fear, fury—I wish to say two things.

First, Christians are not victims and prisoners of either the past or the present. The powers of forgiveness and new creation are at work in their lives. Before them lies a sure and certain hope of deliverance, transformation, and glory. Joy will some day be theirs in fullest measure.

Second, Christians have, so to speak, larger souls than other people; for grief and joy, like desolation and hope, or pain and peace, can coexist in their lives in a way that non-Christians know nothing about. This does not mean that pain ceases to be felt; it means that something else is experienced alongside the hurt. People who sorrow should be told that God offers them joy whatever their circumstances.

Hot Tub Religion, 143-144

REFLECT: Joy and peace can coexist with grief and pain.

It is true that some preach Christ out of envy and rivalry,... not sincerely, supposing that they can stir up trouble for me while I am in chains. But what does it matter? The important thing is that in every way, whether from false motives or true, Christ is preached. And because of this I rejoice.

Philippians 1:15, 17-18

Note how Paul reacts. It would have been easy for him to slip into the spineless self-pity and nail-biting misery that his rivals were wishing upon him. He knew, however, what every one of us needs to know: we are free not to choose the feelings that others choose for us. So he declines to feel miserable. How do we react when meanness and malice link arms to create misery? How do we cope when we find ourselves surrounded by people who want to pull us down? From Paul's example we learn that even at such times joy and peace are possible. We do not have to react as others want us to react. To a greater extent than we may yet have realized, we can choose what to think about. If we focus our mind on joy-inducing facts, we become impervious to those who would plunge us into misery, however great their hostility, however strong their influence, and however little we can do about them.

Hot Tub Religion, 147-148

REFLECT: Joy is a choice.

Rejoice in the Lord always. I will say it again: Rejoice!
Philippians 4:4

Joy is one aspect of the fruit of the Spirit, and the habit of rejoicing in the Lord, as the appointed means whereby joy becomes a reality, is a matter of divine command and Christian duty. It is true that joy, both natural and spiritual, will periodically come upon us as a gust or glow of unsought exhilaration, an unexpected kiss from heaven as it were, for which we should be grateful every time; but we are not on that account to think of joy as essentially a mood of euphoria for which we ask and then sit down to wait. Joy is a habit of the heart, induced and sustained as an abiding quality of one's life through the discipline of rejoicing. Joy is not an accident of temperament or an unpredictable providence; joy is a matter of choice. Paul is directing his readers to choose to rejoice because it is in and through the activity of rejoicing that joy becomes a personal reality.

Hot Tub Religion, 164-165

REFLECT: Joy is a habit.

May all who seek you
rejoice and be glad in you;
may those who love your salvation always say,
"The LORD be exalted!"
Yet I am poor and needy;
may the Lord think of me.

Psalm 40:16-17

Joy is not the same thing as jollity, that is, the cheerful exuberance of the person who is always the life of the party, the one who can be relied on for jokes and general effervescence and of whom people say that there's never a dull moment when he or she is around. Some Christians are like that, others are not and never will be, but this is a matter of temperament that has nothing to do with joy. One may have a bouncy temperament and yet miss joy, or one may be a low-key person with a melancholic streak and yet have joy in abundance. That is good news, for if joy depended on having a jolly temperament, half my readers, and I with them, would have to conclude ourselves unqualified and debarred from joy forever. But the truth is that however our temperaments differ, the life of "joy in the Lord" is available to us all.

Hot Tub Religion, 151

REFLECT: Joy can be mine, whatever my natural temperament.

It is good and proper for a man to eat and drink, and to find satisfaction in his toilsome labor under the sun during the few days of life God has given him—for this is his lot.

Ecclesiastes 5:18

Joy is not the same thing as being carefree. Advertisements that picture nubile young adults sprawling all over the Bahamas seek to persuade us that "getting away from it all" on vacation is the recipe for joy. Many people agree. But if that is so, as soon as the vacation ends and you return to the responsibilities and burdens and abrasivenesses of life—the depressing workplace, the uncongenial company, the repeated disappointments—joy will end because you are no longer carefree. Joy, on this view, will only be available to us for our two- or three-week vacation each year! This is the escapist idea of joy; we should be thankful that it is not true.

Hot Tub Religion, 152

REFLECT: Joy comes, if at all, in the midst of my daily experiences.

The kingdom of God is not a matter of eating and drinking, but of righteousness, peace and joy in the Holy Spirit.

Romans 14:17

Joy makes you shout; joy makes you jump; joy turns mere existence into real living. Joy produces tears, and when you weep for joy, it is not because you are miserable. I remember my son at the age of seven or eight rolling around the floor with his eyes full of tears, saying, "I'm so happy! I'm so happy!" Why was this? For the first time in his life he had beaten his daddy at Ping-Pong®! We talk about the joys of childhood, but there is no reason why joy of equal intensity should not be part of adult life. Joy is at the heart of satisfied living. It is also at the heart of real and credible Christianity, the Christianity that glorifies God and shakes the world. A joyless Christianity (and joylessness cannot be hidden) will become an obstacle to believing, whereas a joyful Christianity is a most arresting advertisement for the transforming power of the gospel.

Hot Tub Religion, 140-142

REFLECT: Joy is at the heart of believable Christianity.

DECEMBER

God wills to live
eternally with us.

This man was handed over to you by God's set purpose and fore-knowledge; and you, with the help of wicked men, put him to death by nailing him to the cross. But God raised him from the dead, freeing him from the agony of death, because it was impossible for death to keep its hold on him.

Acts 2:23-24

The Bible's dominant conviction about God, a conviction proclaimed from Genesis to Revelation, is that behind and beneath all the apparent confusion of this world lies his plan. That plan concerns the perfecting of a people and the restoring of a world through the mediating action of Christ. God governs human affairs with this end in view. His plan cannot be thwarted by human sin, because God made a way for human sin itself to be a part of the plan. The cross of Christ is the supreme illustration of this principle. At Calvary God overruled human sin, which he foresaw, as a means of salvation of the world. Thus it appears that human lawlessness does not thwart God's plan for his people's redemption. Rather, through the wisdom of omnipotence, it has become the means of fulfilling that plan.

Hot Tub Religion, 15-17

REFLECT: Human sin cannot finally overthrow God's plan.

Praise be to the God and Father of our Lord Jesus Christ! In his great mercy he has given us new birth into a living hope through the resurrection of Jesus Christ from the dead.

1 Peter 1:3

God made us hoping creatures, creatures who live very much in their own future, creatures whose nature it is to look forward, and to get excited about good things that we foresee, and to draw joy and strength to cope with the present from our expectations of future fulfillment and delight. We say, "While there's life, there's hope." But the deeper truth is that while there is hope, there is life, because in the absence of anything exciting to look forward to, life no longer feels worth living. Jesus Christ himself, to whom we who believe are united even now, is the Christian's hope. Each of us is traveling along a path that he has appointed for us to an eternity of joy in which he will be the center, the focus, and the source of our endless delight.

Rediscovering Holiness, 247-248

REFLECT: Jesus Christ, the Christian's hope, gives endless life.

We always thank God, the Father of our Lord Jesus Christ, when we pray for you, because we have heard of your faith in Christ Jesus and of the love you have for all the saints—the faith and love that spring from the hope that is stored up for you in heaven.

Colossians 1:3-5

Christianity sees each person as designed for a life beyond this life—an endless life which for those who know God will be far richer and more joyous than our present life can be, and for which life in this world was always meant to be a preparation. The Christian valuation of personal spiritual welfare as more important than any socioeconomic benefit depends ultimately on the knowledge that this world passes away, while the world to come is eternal. We were never intended to treat this world as home, or live in it as if we would be here forever; Jesus pictured the person who lives that way as a fool. It is the way of human nature as God designed it to live in and by one's hopes, and part of the real Christian's joy, increasing with age, is to look forward to eternal life in resurrection glory with the Father and the Son.

"A Christian View of Man," 115-116

REFLECT: This life is preparation for eternal life.

Show me, O LORD, my life's end
and the number of my days;
let me know how fleeting is my life.
You have made my days a mere handbreadth;
the span of my years is as nothing before you.
Each man's life is but a breath.

Psalm 39:4-5

The Puritans have taught me to see and feel the transitoriness of this life, to think of it, with all its richness, as essentially the gymnasium and dressing room where we are prepared for heaven, and to regard readiness to die as the first step in learning to live. The Puritans experienced systematic persecution for their faith; what we today think of as the comforts of home were unknown to them; their medicine and surgery were rudimentary; they had no social security or insurance; it was a world in which more than half the adult population died young and more than half the children born died in infancy, and where disease, distress, discomfort, pain, and death were their constant companions. They would have been lost had they not kept their eyes on heaven and known themselves as pilgrims traveling home to the Celestial City.

"What the Puritans Taught Me," 45

REFLECT: Life is short and often painful; heaven is my true home.

Do you not know that in a race all the runners run, but only one gets the prize? Run in such a way as to get the prize.

1 Corinthians 9:24

Ever since I read Richard Baxter's sprawling, rhapsodic classic, *The Saints' Everlasting Rest*, forty years ago, I have thought that today's Christians ought to be much more heavenly minded than we are. Baxter showed me how the hope of heaven should spur us to resolute effort in our discipleship and also bring us joy, since heaven is our real home. When persons suffering loss of memory cannot recall where their earthly home is, we pity them; but Christians who forget that heaven is their true home, and never think positively about heaven at all, are much more to be pitied.

Aging Christians like me need to hear a lot about heaven; for knowing what you have to look forward to, and actually looking forward to it, keeps you alive inside, whatever the state of your body. If the prospect of being with Jesus Christ, closer than ever before—all frustration, weakness, and pain having been left behind—does not thrill us constantly, our Christianity is dreadfully substandard. If we really loved our Lord, would not this guaranteed hope be a source of eager delight?

"Why I Like My Pie in the Sky," 11

REFLECT: The hope of heaven promotes discipleship and brings joy.

A voice says, "Cry out."
And I said, "What shall I cry?"
"All men are like grass,
and all their glory is like the flowers of the field.
The grass withers and the flowers fall,
because the breath of the LORD blows on them.
Surely the people are grass."

Isaiah 40:6-7

Dr. Johnson is credited with the remark that when a man knows he is going to be hanged in a fortnight it concentrates his mind wonderfully. In the same way, the Puritans' awareness that in the midst of life we are in death, just one step from eternity, gave them a deep seriousness, calm yet passionate, with regard to the business of living that Christians in today's opulent, mollycoddled, earthbound Western world rarely manage to match. Few of us live daily on the edge of eternity in the conscious way that the Puritans did, and we lose out as a result. For the extraordinary vivacity, even hilarity (yes, hilarity), with which the Puritans lived stemmed directly, I believe, from the unflinching, matter-of-fact realism with which they prepared themselves for death, so as always to be found, as it were, packed up and ready to go. The knowledge that God would eventually decide, without consulting them, when their work on earth was done brought energy for the work itself while they were still being given time to get on with it.

"What the Puritans Taught Me," 45-46

REFLECT: In the midst of life, I am in death.

Teach us to number our days aright,
that we may gain a heart of wisdom.

Psalm 90:12

Creative Christian thought about spiritual life is now fun-neled almost entirely into exploring spiritual and relational enrichment in this world. We preach to each other, and write books for each other, about the path to present blessings in its various forms, and heaven and hell hardly get a mention. We treat any call to think seriously about the world to come, not as a sober Christian realism, based on Scripture, but as a sign either of escapism, if the focus is on heaven, or of vindic-tiveness, if it is on hell. The wisdom, received from the Christian past, that only when one is ready to die is one ready to live, is forgotten; with the world, we treat continuance of life, as such, as the supreme value. Death finds us unpre-pared, and in daily life it is observable how little strength we have for the practice of detachment or renunciation in any form at all. Authentic spirituality, however, requires of us that we relearn the discipline of setting loose everything here in order to lay hold of glory hereafter.

"Evangelicals and the Way of Salvation," 156

REFLECT: A Christian realist takes the next world more seriously than this one.

All can see that wise men die; the foolish and the senseless alike perish and leave their wealth to others.... But God will redeem my life from the grave; he will surely take me to himself.

Psalm 49:10, 15

In every century until our own, Christians saw this life as preparation for eternity. Medievals, Puritans, and later evangelicals thought and wrote much about the art of dying well, and urged that all life should be seen as preparation for leaving it behind. This was not otiose morbidity, but realistic wisdom, since death really is the one certain fact of life. Acting the ostrich with regard to it is folly to the highest degree. Yet today it has become conventional to think as if we are all going to live in this world forever and to view every case of bereavement as a reason for doubting the goodness of God. We must all know, deep down, that this is ridiculous, but we do it all the same. And in doing it we part company with the Bible, with historic Christianity, and with a basic principle of right living. Dag Hammarskjöld was thinking Christianly when he wrote that no philosophy that cannot make sense of death can make sense of life either.

"Dying Well Is Final Test," 46

REFLECT: Only when I know how to die can I know how to live.

Paul answered, "Why are you weeping and breaking my heart? I am ready not only to be bound, but also to die in Jerusalem for the name of the Lord Jesus."

Acts 21:13

Since believers do not know when Christ will come for them, readiness to leave this world at any time is vital Christian wisdom. Each day should find us like children looking forward to their holidays, who get packed up and ready to go a long time in advance. The formula for readiness is "Live each day as if thy last" (Thomas Ken)—in other words, keep short accounts with God. Dying well is one of the good works to which Christians are called, and Christ will enable us who serve him to die well, however gruesome the physical process itself. And dying thus, in Christ, through Christ, and with Christ, will be a spiritual blossoming.

"Dying Well Is Final Test," 46

REFLECT: I need to be ready to meet Christ.

Brothers, we do not want you to be ignorant about those who fall asleep, or to grieve like the rest of men, who have no hope.

1 Thessalonians 4:13

We look on death as an exit, a way out from the light we love into a hateful darkness. So it is for unbelievers, but for Christians death is an entrance, a way leading from twilight here (spiritually, life here is never more than that) into the sunshine of seeing our God. A Christian's death is promotion, not tragedy, however early in life it comes; the mourners weep for themselves and for those left behind. When Bunyan's Christiana died, "her Children wept, but Mr. Great-heart, and Mr. Valiant"—two men of faith who know what death was about—"played upon the well-tuned Cymbal and Harp for Joy." "If we knew what God knows about death," said George MacDonald, "we would clap our hands."

Growing in Christ, 148

REFLECT: When Christians die, they enter into God's presence.

Do not let your hearts be troubled. Trust in God; trust also in me. In my Father's house are many rooms; if it were not so, I would have told you. I am going there to prepare a place for you. And if I go and prepare a place for you, I will come back and take you to be with me that you also may be where I am.

John 14:1-3

Physical death is the outward sign of that eternal separation from God which is the Creator's judgment on sin, and which will only become deeper and more painful through the milestone event of dying, unless saving grace intervenes. Unconverted people do well therefore to fear death: it is in truth fearsome. For Christians, however, death's sting is withdrawn. Grace has intervened, and now their death day becomes an appointment with their Savior, who will be there to take them to the rest prepared for them. Though they will be temporarily bodiless, which is not good, they will be closer to Christ than ever before, "which is better by far" (Philippians 1:23).

"Dying Well Is Final Test," 46

REFLECT: Christians have no need to fear death.

Father, I want those you have given me to be with me where I am, and to see my glory, the glory you have given me because you loved me before the creation of the world.

John 17:24

On a day entered from eternity in God's private calendar, my heart is due to stop beating. When or how it will happen I do not know. All I know is that some day, some way, my heart will stop, and what the world will call my death-day will really be a birthday—the third in line. What were my other two birthdays? Number one was when I left the womb, to see and feel and feed and shout as an inhabitant of this physical world; number two was when I came from spiritual darkness eighteen years later to see and feel and feed and shout about God's salvation and Christ's love for me. By "birthday," you see, I mean not an anniversary but a day that sees me start enjoying gifts of God such as I had never before imagined. Said D. L. Moody, "Someday they'll tell you Moody's dead. Don't you believe it! That day I'll be before the throne; I'll be more alive than I've ever been." That is why my death-day will truly be a birthday.

Growing in Christ, 147-148

REFLECT: For a Christian, death is another step in enjoying God's gifts.

If I fought wild beasts in Ephesus for merely human reasons, what have I gained? If the dead are not raised, "Let us eat and drink, for tomorrow we die."

1 Corinthians 15:32

Death is the fundamental human problem, for if death is really final, nothing is worthwhile save self-indulgence. No philosophy or religion which cannot come to terms with death is any real use to us. Here, however, Christianity stands out. Alone among the world's faiths and "isms" it views death as conquered. For Christian faith is hope resting on fact—namely, the fact that Jesus rose bodily from the grave and now lives eternally in heaven. The hope is that when Jesus comes back—the day when history stops and this world ends—he "will transform our lowly bodies so that they will be like his glorious body" (Philippians 3:21). Ask God to show you how Jesus' life, body and soul, was the only fully human life that has ever been lived, and keep looking at Jesus, as you meet him in the Gospels, till you can see it. Then the prospect of being like him—that, and no less—will seem to you the noblest and most magnificent destiny possible, and by embracing it you will become a true disciple.

Growing in Christ, 83-84, 86

REFLECT: Christian faith is hope of eternal life resting on the fact of Jesus' resurrection and life in heaven.

Now we know that if the earthly tent we live in is destroyed, we have a building from God, an eternal house in heaven, not built by human hands. Meanwhile we groan... and are burdened, because we do not wish to be unclothed but to be clothed with our heavenly dwelling, so that what is mortal may be swallowed up by life.

2 Corinthians 5:1-2, 4

Death is gain for believers because after death they are closer to Christ. At death the souls of believers are made perfect in holiness and enter into the worshiping life of heaven. But disembodiment, as such, is not gain; bodies are for expression and experience, and to be without a body is to be impoverished. This is why Paul wants to be "clothed" with his resurrection body rather than be "unclothed" (that is, disembodied). To be resurrected for the life of heaven is the true Christian hope. As life in the "intermediate" state between death and resurrection is better than the life in this world that preceded it, so the life of resurrection will be better still. It will, in fact, be best. And this is what God has in store for all his children. Hallelujah!

Concise Theology, 248-249

REFLECT: In the life of resurrection, both my body and my soul will be made perfect in holiness.

The Lord himself will come down from heaven, with a loud command, with the voice of the archangel and with the trumpet call of God, and the dead in Christ will rise first. After that, we who are still alive... will be caught up together with them in the clouds to meet the Lord in the air.

1 Thessalonians 4:16-17

Christ will return to this world in glory. Jesus comes to end history, to raise the dead and judge the world, to impart to God's children their final glory, and to usher in a reconstructed universe. The return of Christ will have the same significance for Christians who will be alive when it happens as death has for Christians who die before it happens: it will be the end of life in this world and the start of life in what has been described as "an unknown environment with a well-known inhabitant." Christ teaches that it will be a tragic disaster if his coming finds anyone in an unprepared state. Rather, the thought of what is to come should be constantly on our minds, encouraging us in our present Christian service and teaching us to live as it were on call, ready to go to meet Christ at any time.

Concise Theology, 250-253

REFLECT: My life now is a preparation to meet Christ in glory.

Listen, I tell you a mystery: We will not all sleep, but we will all be changed—in a flash, in the twinkling of an eye, at the last trumpet. For the trumpet will sound, the dead will be raised imperishable, and we will be changed.

1 Corinthians 15:51-52

Jesus was the first to rise from the dead, and when he returns to this world he will raise his servants to a resurrection life like his own. Christians alive at his coming will at that instant undergo a marvelous transformation, while Christians who had died will experience a glorious re-embodiment. The bodies that Christians have now are at best poor tools for expressing the desires and purposes of regenerate hearts, and many of the weaknesses with which the saints struggle—shyness, shortness of temper, lust, depression, coolness in relationships, and so on—are closely linked with our physical constitution and its patterning in our behavior. The bodies that become ours in the general resurrection will be bodies that perfectly match our perfected regenerate characters and will prove perfect instruments for our holy self-expression throughout eternity.

Concise Theology, 254-256

REFLECT: At Jesus' second coming, I will receive a fully functional new body.

So will it be with the resurrection of the dead. The body that is sown is perishable, it is raised imperishable; it is sown in dis - honor, it is raised in glory; it is sown in weakness, it is raised in power; it is sown a natural body, it is raised a spiritual body.

1 Corinthians 15:42-44

Glorification is a work of transforming power whereby God finally turns us into sinless creatures in deathless bodies. The idea of our glorified final state includes (a) perfect knowledge of grace, through limitless extension of our powers of understanding; (b) perfect enjoyment of seeing and being with the Father and the Son; (c) perfect worship and service of God out of a perfectly integrated nature and a heart set perfectly free for love and obedience; (d) perfect deliverance from all that is experienced as sinful, evil, weakening, and frustrating; (e) perfect fulfillment of all desires of which we are conscious; (f) perfect completion of all that was good and valuable in this world's life but that had to be left incomplete because desire outran capacity; and (g) endless personal growth in the encompassing of all these perfect things.

Concise Theology, 256-257

REFLECT: God's ultimate will for me is perfection.

Do not be deceived: God cannot be mocked. A man reaps what he sows.

Galatians 6:7

New Testament Christianity is essentially two-worldly: not other-worldly in the sense of lacking interest in this world, but seeing life here as travel to, and preparation for, and indeed a foretaste of, a life hereafter in which all without exception will reap what they sowed here in terms of their attitude and decision Godward. Death, or the return of Jesus Christ, whichever comes first, will effect a transition from the world of life choices to the world where our Maker gives us what, fundamentally, we choose concerning him—either to be eternally with him, or eternally without him. And since our experience of the destiny we chose will be unending, and will in fact grow directly out of our life now, the whole of this present life should be lived in light of the future—which means, for Christians, living in the power of the magnificent hope of glory with Christ that the Father has given them.

"Evangelicals and the Way of Salvation," 155

REFLECT: In the next life, I receive what I chose in this life.

I heard what sounded like the roar of a great multitude in heaven shouting: "Hallelujah! Salvation and glory and power belong to our God, for true and just are his judgments. He has condemned the great prostitute who corrupted the earth by her adulteries.... Hallelujah! The smoke from her goes up for ever and ever."

Revelation 19:1-3

When Christians get to heaven, with their sanctification complete and their minds as fully conformed to the mind of Christ as the angels' minds are, they will forever rejoice not only in the mercies by which God has glorified himself in their own lives, but also in the judgments by which he vindicates himself against those who defy him. Christians sometimes find this hard to believe because, being at present imperfectly sanctified sinners themselves, they have so much fellow feeling for other sinners, and as yet so little sense of how God is glorified in his retributive judgments. But there can be no doubt that learning to praise God properly for his judgments, no less than for his mercies, is something that all the saints have to look forward to, as part of God's schooling of them in the life of holiness.

A Passion for Faithfulness, 102

REFLECT: God's judgments on all who defy his will and corrupt the earth are just.

God "will give to each person according to what he has done."
Romans 2:6

At the judgment all will give account of themselves to God. The regenerate, who as servants of Christ have learned to love righteousness and desire the glory of a holy heaven, will be acknowledged, and on the basis of Christ's atonement and merit on their behalf they will be awarded that which they seek. The rest will receive a destiny commensurate with the godless way of life they have chosen, and that destiny will come to them on the basis of their own demerit. How much they knew of the will of God will be the standard by which their demerit is assessed. The judgment will demonstrate, and so finally vindicate, the perfect justice of God. In a world of sinners, it is no wonder that evil is rampant and that doubts arise as to whether God, if sovereign, can be just, or if just, can be sovereign. But for God to judge justly is his glory, and the Last Judgment will be his final self-vindication against the suspicion that he has ceased to care about righteousness.

Concise Theology, 259

REFLECT: I will be judged on the basis of either Christ's merit or my own failings.

Whoever believes in him is not condemned, but whoever does not believe stands condemned already because he has not believed in the name of God's one and only Son.

John 3:18

Scripture sees hell as self-chosen; those in hell will realize that they sentenced themselves to it by loving darkness rather than light, choosing not to have their Creator as their Lord, preferring self-indulgent sin to self-denying righteousness, and (if they encountered the gospel) rejecting Jesus rather than coming to him. From this standpoint hell appears as God's gesture of respect for human choice. All receive what they actually chose, either to be with God forever, worshiping him, or without God forever, worshiping themselves. Those who are in hell will know not only that for their doings they deserve it but also that in their hearts they chose it.

The purpose of Bible teaching about hell is to make us appreciate, thankfully embrace, and rationally prefer the grace of Christ that saves us from it. It is really a mercy to mankind that God in Scripture is so explicit about hell. We cannot now say that we have not been warned.

Concise Theology, 262-263

REFLECT: Hell is God's gesture of respect for human choice.

The Lord is not slow in keeping his promise, as some understand slowness. He is patient with you, not wanting anyone to perish, but everyone to come to repentance.

2 Peter 3:9

Does not the existence of evil—moral badness, useless pain, and waste of good—suggest that God the Father is not almighty after all—for surely he would remove these things if he could? Yes, he would, and he is doing so! Through Christ, bad folk like you and me are already being made good; new pain-and-disease-free bodies are on the way, and a reconstructed cosmos with them. If God moves more slowly than we wish in clearing evil out of his world and introducing the new order, that, we may be sure, is in order to widen his gracious purpose and include in it more victims of the world's evil than otherwise he could have done.

Growing in Christ, 33

REFLECT: God is at work removing evil from the universe.

Then the end will come, when he hands over the kingdom to God the Father after he has destroyed all dominion, authority and power. For he must reign until he has put all his enemies under his feet. The last enemy to be destroyed is death.

1 Corinthians 15:24-26

In overruling and using moral evil for his own good ends, and so making it part of his plan, God remains innocent of blame for the evil itself. Guilt and blame belong to the rebel creatures who deliberately defy their Creator. So much Scripture makes clear, though without attempting to tell us all that was and is involved in God's sovereign decisions concerning sin—his decisions, that is, that have allowed and do allow to happen that which he hates and forbids. We need to remember that we only know about God what he tells us; speculation gets us nowhere except into bewilderment, confusion, and error. As we think about this, we can bear in mind that God is now at work in and through Christ to eliminate the evil that for the moment he permits, within set limits, to exist, and he will not give up until all evil has become a thing of the past.

"Westminster and the Roller Coaster Ride," 9-10

REFLECT: One day God will completely destroy all traces of evil.

You died, and your life is now hidden with Christ in God.
Colossians 3:3

In a weary world in which grave philosophers were counseling suicide as man's best option, the unshakable, rollicking optimism of the first Christians, who went on feeling on top of the world however much the world seemed to be on top of them, made a vast impression. It still does, when Christians are Christian enough to show it! Christians enjoy here and now a hidden life of fellowship with the Father and the Son which nothing, not even death itself, can touch—for it is the life of the world to come begun already, the life of heaven tasted here on earth. The explanation of this experience, which all God's people know in some measure, is that believers have actually passed through death (not as a physical but as a personal and psychic event) into the eternal life which lies beyond.

Growing in Christ, 64-66

REFLECT: As a believer in Christ, I have passed from death into eternal life.

When the time had fully come, God sent his Son, born of a woman, born under law, to redeem those under law, that we might receive the full rights of sons.

Galatians 4:4-5

The Bible details the stages of God's plan. God visited Abraham, led him into Canaan, and entered into a covenant relationship with him and his descendants. He turned Abraham's family into a nation and led them out of Egypt into a land of their own. Over the centuries he prepared them and the Gentile world for the coming of the Savior-King. At last, God sent his Son to redeem us, "so that we might receive the full rights of sons." The covenant promise to Abraham's seed is now fulfilled to all who put faith in Christ. The plan for this age is that this gospel should be known throughout the world. Then, at Christ's return, heaven and earth will in some unimaginable way be remade and, in God's presence, "his servants will serve him. They will see his face, ... and they will reign for ever and ever" (Revelation 22:3-5). This is the plan of God, says the Bible.

Hot Tub Religion, 15-16

REFLECT: Jesus' birth was at the heart of God's plan to remake the world.

*Oh, the depth of the riches of the wisdom and knowledge of God!
How unsearchable his judgments, and his paths beyond tracing
out! For from him and through him and to him are all things.
To him be the glory forever! Amen.*

Romans 11:33, 36

The plan of salvation teaches me, not merely that I can
never do anything to earn, increase, or extend God's favor, or
to avoid the justified fury of his wrath, or to wheedle benefits
out of him, but also that I never need to try to do any of
these things. God himself has loved me from eternity. He
himself has redeemed me from hell through the cross. He
himself has renewed my heart and brought me to faith. He
himself has now sovereignly committed himself to complete
the transformation of me into Christ's likeness and to set me,
faultless and glorified, in his own presence for all eternity.
When almighty love has thus totally taken over the task of
getting me home to glory, responsive love, fed by gratitude
and expressed in thanksgiving, should surface spontaneously
as the ruling passion of my life. It will be my wisdom to
brood on and mull over the marvelous mercies of God's plan
until it does.

Rediscovering Holiness, 75-76

REFLECT: God has loved me from eternity and will continue to love me forever.

You have come to Mount Zion, to the heavenly Jerusalem, the city of the living God. You have come to thousands upon thousands of angels in joyful assembly, to the church of the firstborn, whose names are written in heaven. You have come to God, the judge of all men, to the spirits of righteous men made perfect, to Jesus the mediator of a new covenant.

Hebrews 12:22-24

Heaven is infinitely more important than the present life, not only because it is endless while this life is temporary, but also because no relationships are perfectly enjoyed here in the way that they will be hereafter. From the fact that the Holy Trinity is the ultimate reality, no less than from the insights of present-day psychologists, we learn that relationships are what life is really all about, and relationships, with Father, Son, and saints, are certainly what heaven is all about. Heaven will be an experience of *togetherness,* closer and more joyous than any we have known so far.

But for perfect communion not only must God give without limit or restraint; his servants, angelic and human, must also respond without reserve—which means that in and through them God's will is fully done. The doing of God's will is thus part of the definition of heaven, and it is part of heaven's glory that God gives those who are there full ability to do it.

Growing in Christ, 184-185

REFLECT: In heaven I will be fully able to do God's will.

"They will build houses and dwell in them;
they will plant vineyards and eat their fruit....
The wolf and the lamb will feed together,
and the lion will eat straw like the ox....
They will neither harm nor destroy
on all my holy mountain," says the LORD.

Isaiah 65:21, 25

What shall we do in heaven? Not lounge around!—but worship, work, think, and communicate, enjoying activity, beauty, people, and God. First and foremost, we shall see and love Jesus, our Savior, Master, and Friend. I have been writing with enthusiasm, for this everlasting life is something to which I look forward. Why? Not because I am out of love with life here—just the reverse! My life is full of joy, from four sources—knowing God, and people, and the good and pleasant things that God and men under God have created, and doing things which are worthwhile for God or others or for myself as God's man. As I get older, I find that I appreciate God, and people, and good and lovely and noble things more and more intensely; so it is pure delight to think that this enjoyment will continue and increase in some form, literally forever.

Growing in Christ, 88-89

REFLECT: The life of heaven will continue and increase my joy on earth.

The throne of God and of the Lamb will be in the city, and his servants will serve him. They will see his face, and his name will be on their foreheads. There will be no more night. They will not need the light of a lamp or the light of the sun, for the Lord God will give them light.

Revelation 22:3-5

Once I stood on top of Ben Nevis, Britain's highest point, with gray mist everywhere, so that I could not see a thing. (It had been like that all the way up.) But when I raised my head the mist above me gleamed so bright that it hurt my eyes. Clearly there were only a few feet of it between me and the sun. The intensity of my longing in that moment that the mist might roll away was painful. (Alas, it didn't; I shall have to climb Ben Nevis again.) Some of Scripture's achingly beautiful pictures of heaven stir Christian hearts in a similar way: like the glowing mist, they give a sense of the nearness of the sun that you cannot see (which in this case is the Son) and arouse the wish to be fully in the brightness beyond the mist. On Ben Nevis I wanted to see the sun; on earth the Christians hope with strong desire for the day when they will see their Lord.

God's Words, 28

REFLECT: In heaven I will see God face to face.

Blessed are the pure in heart, for they will see God.

Matthew 5:8

The essence of heavenly reward will be more of what the Christian desires most, namely, a deepening of his or her love relationship with the Savior, which is the reality to which all the biblical imagery of honorific crowns and robes and feasts is pointing. The reward is parallel to the reward of courtship, which is the enriching of the love relationship itself through marriage. So the life of heavenly glory is a compound of seeing God in and through Christ and being loved by the Father and the Son, of rest and work, of praise and worship, and of fellowship with the Lamb and the saints. The hearts of those in heaven say, "I want this to go on forever." And it will. There can be no better news than this.

Concise Theology, 266-267

REFLECT: Heaven is never-ending fellowship with Christ.

I am convinced that neither death nor life, neither angels nor demons, neither the present nor the future, nor any powers, neither height nor depth, nor anything else in all creation, will be able to separate us from the love of God that is in Christ Jesus our Lord.

Romans 8:38-39

The Christian under grace is free from bondage to fear—fear, that is, of the unknown future, or of meeting God (as one day we all must do), or of being destroyed by hostile forces or horrific experiences of one sort or another. He knows himself to be God's child, adopted, beloved, secure, with his inheritance awaiting him and eternal joy guaranteed. He knows that nothing can separate him from the love of God in Christ, nor dash him from his Savior's hand, and that nothing can happen to him which is not for his long-term good, making him more like Jesus and bringing him ultimately closer to his God. So when fears flood his soul, as they do the soul of every normal person from time to time, he drives them back by reminding himself of God's amazing grace.

God's Words, 107

REFLECT: By God's grace, I will enjoy his love in Christ forever.

BIBLICAL REFERENCES

BIBLICAL REFERENCES

BIBLICAL REFERENCES

John 12:24	October 10	Romans 12:10	April 4
John 12:26	September 15	Romans 13:9-10	August 20
John 14:1-3	December 11	Romans 14:10	April 21
John 14:26	November 2	Romans 14:13	November 6
John 15:9-10	November 23	Romans 14:17	November 30
John 15:11	August 29	Romans 15:13	November 18
John 16:13-14	September 3	Romans 15:17-18	May 2
John 16:32-33	October 7		
John 17:15, 18	June 14	1 Corinthians 1:4	March 29
John 17:24	December 12	1 Corinthians 1:12-13	April 18
John 20:21	June 20	1 Corinthians 1:27	October 19
John 21:15	June 18	1 Corinthians 3:6-7	June 5
		1 Corinthians 6:12	July 24
Acts 2:23-24	December 1	1 Corinthians 8:9	July 23
Acts 2:37-38	September 4	1 Corinthians 9:24	December 5
Acts 2:42	April 12	1 Corinthians 9:25	November 12
Acts 15:1-2	April 8	1 Corinthians 9:27	April 17
Acts 17:19-21	November 13	1 Corinthians 10:11	February 18
Acts 20:32	April 5	1 Corinthians 10:12	November 9
Acts 21:13	December 9	1 Corinthians 10:13	October 8
Acts 24:16	February 14	1 Corinthians 10:31	July 27
Acts 26:17-18	November 14	1 Corinthians 13:4-7	June 19
		1 Corinthians 15:9-10	March 31
Romans 1:13	April 28	1 Corinthians 15:24-26	December 23
Romans 1:16	June 6	1 Corinthians 15:32	December 13
Romans 1:19-21	February 7	1 Corinthians 15:42-44	December 17
Romans 2:5	August 12	1 Corinthians 15:51-52	December 16
Romans 2:6	December 20		
Romans 3:23-24	March 2	2 Corinthians 1:3-4	October 11
Romans 5:8	March 11	2 Corinthians 3:18	September 5
Romans 5:10-11	March 28	2 Corinthians 4:6	September 17
Romans 6:4-5	September 7	2 Corinthians 4:8-10	October 17
Romans 6:17	August 14	2 Corinthians 4:11	October 20
Romans 7:18-19	March 1	2 Corinthians 4:17	October 3
Romans 8:13	March 27	2 Corinthians 5:1-2, 4	December 14
Romans 8:14	April 26	2 Corinthians 5:14-15	March 14
Romans 8:28-29	September 27	2 Corinthians 5:17	September 6
Romans 8:38-39	December 31	2 Corinthians 10:12	April 20
Romans 9:15-16	April 3	2 Corinthians 12:8-9	May 30
Romans 9:18	May 7	2 Corinthians 13:5	January 16
Romans 9:19	May 8		
Romans 11:33, 36	December 26	Galatians 1:3-5	January 28
Romans 12:1	August 4	Galatians 2:20	August 31
Romans 12:2	January 18	Galatians 4:4-5	December 25
Romans 12:3	October 21	Galatians 5:1	September 9
Romans 12:6-8	June 11	Galatians 5:6	August 3

BIBLICAL REFERENCES

James 1:5, 17	February 1
James 1:6-8	May 27
James 1:21	February 12
James 5:10-11	October 13
James 5:16	April 9
1 Peter 1:1-2	November 1
1 Peter 1:3	December 2
1 Peter 1:13, 15	August 5
1 Peter 2:11-12	August 13
1 Peter 2:16	January 22
1 Peter 2:17	July 4
1 Peter 4:10	April 24
1 Peter 4:19	October 14
1 Peter 5:8	October 6
2 Peter 1:2-3	September 18
2 Peter 1:19	February 3
2 Peter 1:20-21	February 13
2 Peter 3:1-2	February 15
2 Peter 3:9	December 22
2 Peter 3:17-18	November 15
1 John 1:1, 4	November 20
1 John 1:8	November 8
1 John 1:9	March 15
1 John 2:15-17	July 14
1 John 3:4	March 8
1 John 4:1	January 12
1 John 4:19	June 15
1 John 5:2	August 19
1 John 5:20	February 16
2 John 6	November 24
2 John 7	March 5
3 John 2	October 16
Revelation 19:1-3	December 19
Revelation 21:5	January 29
Revelation 22:3-5	December 29

BIBLIOGRAPHY

"Accidie Will Happen." *Pastoral Renewal*, May 1986, 159-60.

"A Bad Trip." *Christianity Today*, March 7, 1986, 12.

"Bringing the Double Mind to Singleness of Faith." *Eternity*, November 1988, 59.

"The Christian and God's World." In *Transforming Our World*, edited by J.M. Boice, 81-97. Portland, Ore.: Multnomah, 1988.

"Christian Gravitas in a Narcissistic Age." *Eternity*, July/August 1988, 46.

"Christian Morality Adrift." In *A Society in Peril*, edited by Kevin Perrotta and John C. Blattner, 57-76. Ann Arbor, Mich.: Servant, 1989.

"A Christian View of Man." In *The Christian Vision: Man in Society*, edited by Lynne Morris, 101-19. Hillsdale, Mich.: Hillsdale College Press, 1984.

Concise Theology. Wheaton, Ill.: Tyndale, 1993.

"Conscience, Choice and Character." In *Law, Morality and the Bible*, edited by G.J. Wenham and B. Kaye, 168-92. Downers Grove, Ill.: InterVarsity Press, 1978.

"Decadence à la Mode." *Christianity Today*, October 2, 1987, 13.

"The Devil's Dossier." *Christianity Today*, June 21, 1993, 24.

"Divisions in the Church." In *The Church: God's New Society*, 35-44. Philadelphia: Philadelphia Conference on Reformed Theology, 1985.

"Does It Really Matter?" *Eternity*, January 1987, 30.

"Dying Well Is Final Test." *Eternity*, April 1987, 46.

"Evangelicals and the Way of Salvation." In *Evangelical Affirmations*, ed. Kenneth S. Kantzer and Carl F.H. Henry, 107-36. Grand Rapids, Mich.: Zondervan, 1990.

Evangelism and the Sovereignty of God. Downers Grove, Ill.: InterVarsity Press, 1961.

God's Words. Downers Grove, Ill.: InterVarsity Press, 1981.

Growing in Christ. Wheaton, Ill.: Crossway, 1994.

"The Holy Spirit and the Local Congregation." *The Churchman*, June 2, 1964, 98-108.

Hot Tub Religion. Wheaton, Ill.: Tyndale House, Living Books, 1987.

"How Christians Should Understand Themselves." *Eternity*, July/August 1987, 36.

BIBLIOGRAPHY

"How to Recognize a Christian Citizen." *Christianity Today*, April 19, 1985, insert 4.

"Introduction: On Being Serious about the Holy Spirit." In David Wells', *God the Evangelist: How the Holy Spirit Works to Bring Men and Women to Faith*, xi-xvi. Grand Rapids, Mich.: Eerdmans, 1987.

"An Introduction to Systematic Spirituality." *Crux*, March 1990, 2-8.

"Introduction: Why Preach?" In *The Preacher and Preaching*, edited by Samuel T. Logan, 1-29. Phillipsburg, N.J.: Presbyterian & Reformed, 1986.

"Keeping Your Balance: A Christian's Challenge." *Eternity*, January 1988, 18.

"Knowing Notions or Knowing God?" *Pastoral Renewal*, March 1982, 65-68.

"The Means of Growth." *Tenth*, July 1981, 2-11.

"My Path of Prayer." In *My Path of Prayer*, edited by David Hanes, 56-65. Brighton, U.K.: Henry E. Walter, 1981.

"Packer the Picketed Pariah." *Christianity Today*, January 11, 1993, 11.

A Passion for Faithfulness. Wheaton, Ill.: Crossway, 1995.

"Paths of Righteousness." *Eternity*, May 1986, 32-37.

"Pleasure Principles." *Christianity Today*, November 22, 1993, 24-26.

"The Reality Cure." *Christianity Today*, September 14, 1992, 34-35.

"The Reconstitution of Authority." *Crux*, December 1982, 2-12.

Rediscovering Holiness. Ann Arbor, Mich.: Servant, Vine, 1992.

"Shepherds after God's Own Heart." *Faith & Renewal*, November 1990, 12-17.

"Situations and Principles." In *Law, Morality and the Bible*, edited by G.J. Wenham and B. Kaye, 151-67. Downers Grove, Ill.: InterVarsity Press, 1978.

"Soldier, Son, Pilgrim: Christian Know Thyself." *Eternity*, April 1988, 33.

"To All Who Will Come." In *Our Savior God*, edited by J.M. Boice, 179-89. Grand Rapids, Mich.: Baker, 1981.

"True Guidance." *Eternity*, June 1986, 36-39.

"Walking to Emmaus with the Great Physician." *Christianity Today*, April 10, 1981, 20-24.

"The Way of the Weak Is the Only Healthy Way." *Eternity*, November 1987, 28.

BIBLIOGRAPHY

"Westminster and the Roller Coaster Ride." *Tabletalk,* March 1990, 6-10.

"The Whale and the Elephant." *Christianity Today,* October 4, 1993, 11.

"What Do You Mean When You Say God?" *Christianity Today,* September 19, 1986, 27-31.

"What the Puritans Taught Me." *Christianity Today,* October 8, 1990, 44-47.

"Why I Like My Pie in the Sky." *Christianity Today,* June 18, 1990, 11.

"Wisdom along the Way." *Eternity,* April 1986, 19-23.

"The Word of Life." *The Evangelical Catholic,* July/August 1992, 1-8.

A BIBLICAL APPROACH
TO GUIDANCE

1. Live with the question, What is the best I can do for my God?

2. Note the instructions of Scripture: the summons to love God and others, the limits set and the obligations established by the law, the insistence on energetic action (Ecclesiastes 8:10; 1 Corinthians 15:58), the drilling in wisdom to enable one to make the best choice among behavioral options.

3. Follow the examples of godliness in Scripture: most of all, imitate the love and humility of Jesus himself. While that is what we are doing, we cannot go far wrong.

4. Let wisdom judge the best course of action: not only the wisdom that God gives you personally but the corporate wisdom of your friends and guides in the Christian community. Don't be a spiritual lone ranger; when you think you see God's will, have your perception checked. Draw on the wisdom of those who are wiser than you are; take advice.

5. Take note of any nudges from God that come your way—any special concerns for ministry and service, and restlessness of heart which might indicate that something needs to be changed.

6. Cherish the divine peace which, as Paul says, "garrisons" (guards, keeps safe and steady) the hearts of those who are in God's will.

7. Observe the limits set by circumstances to what is possible; and when it is clear that those limits cannot be changed, accept them as from God.

8. Be prepared for God's guidance on a particular issue not to appear until the time comes for decision about it, and for God to guide you one step at a time; for that is how he usually does it.

9. Be prepared to find God directing you to something you thought you would not like, and teaching you to like it!

10. Never forget that if you make a bad decision, it is not the end of everything: God forgives and restores. He is your covenant God and Savior; he will not let you go, however badly you may have slipped. The Lord is my shepherd; he leads me. What a relief it is to know that.

"Wisdom along the Way," 23